I'M STUCK

Help Me Start A Youth Ministry in the African American Church

I'M STUCK

Help Me Start A Youth Ministry
in the
African American Church

By

Dr. Oneal Sandidge

Nashville, Tennessee

Credits

The cover design is by Professor Alexis (Tommy) Joyner, Professor of Art, Elizabeth City State University, Elizabeth City, North Carolina.

Poetry submitted by Rev. Ronnie A. Clark, Lynchburg, Virginia, Mr. Michael D. Williams of New York City, and Mr. Aron Liles, Atlanta, Georgia.

Unless otherwise indicated, Scripture quotations are from the Contemporary English Version of the Bible. Copyright 1991, 1992, 1995 by American Bible Society. Used by permission.

Library of Congress Cataloging in Publication Data

Sandidge, Oneal Cleaven.
    I'm stuck: help me start a youth ministry in the African-Amerian church/ Oneal Sandidge.
        p. cm.
    Includes bibliographical references and index.

ISBN 0-910683-14-X
1. Church work with Afro-American youth. I. Title.
BV4468.2.A34S26 1998   98-40580
259'.23' 08996073—dc21   CIP

Published by Townsend Press
Nashville, Tennessee

Special Thanks

There are many people to thank for this work: Readers who spent much time reading part or the entire manuscript: Rev. Russell Marquis, Youth Pastor of the distinguished Concord Baptist Church, Brooklyn, New York; Dr. Barbara Lucas, Professor of Education and Associate Dean of New York Theological Seminary; Dr. Gloria Taylor, Professor of Christian Education, Virginia Union University, School of Theology; Miss Patty King, Ph.D. English major at Georgia State University, Atlanta, Georgia; Dr. James Campbell, Ph.D., Chair of English Department, Lynchburg College, Lynchburg, Virginia; and Robyn Roberts, journalist; Miss Patricia Spence, Rev. Arlington Medley and Michael D. Williams of New York City. Thanks also to Rev. Richard Stanford, Stone Mountain, Georgia for typing, formatting, and editing services, and Mr. Chris Jackson, writer and author, Antioch, Tennessee.

Encouragement

Many people have encouraged me to write this book: Mr. William K. Hunter, Jr., Mr. Larry D. Hunter, and Mrs. Arlean S. Hunter, all of the Lynchburg, Virginia area; Rev. Ronnie A. Clark, Rev. Anthony Graham of Murfreesboro, Tennessee; Rev. Leroy Minter, Atlanta, Georgia; Rev. William Johnson of Madison Heights, Virginia; Rev. Joseph Moore of Fredericksburg, Virginia; Mr. Aron Liles, Atlanta, Georgia; Mr. Leonard Mason of New York City; Mr. Ernest Haynes, Lynchburg, Virginia; and Mr. Sidney Miller of Richmond, Virginia for traveling assistance.

Dedication

This book is dedicated to the following persons:
* God the Father, Son, and the Holy Spirit
* My deceased father: Mr. Wardie Sandidge
* My mother: Mrs. Hattie Mae Dawson Sandidge
* My wife: Mrs. Janice Cheryl Oliver
* My son: Mr. Jermaine Oneal Sandidge
* My daughter: Miss Ieke Monique Sandidge
* My godson: Rev. Ronnie A. Clark

Comments About This Work

Rev. Sandidge says what many African American churches will not admit, saying what needs to be said about youth ministry in African American churches, "meeting and discussing youth concerns... is not youth ministry, neither is allowing youth to set the agenda. It's much more." Rev. Sandidge tells us how to begin a viable, meaningful, God centered youth ministry.

—Miss Patricia Spence, Superintendent of Church School, Convent Avenue Baptist Church, New York City

"The truths discussed in this manual together with the practical and usable suggestions will be used over and over again. These truths could transform youth ministry into places of dynamic ministry. It is a must reading for youth leaders in the African American church who want the church to be what God intended it to be and who want to invest in the spiritual and social security of our youth."

—Deaconess Eloise Blake, Chair, Board of Christian Education, Convent Avenue Baptist Church, New York, New York

"If you're looking for helpful hints in structuring your youth ministry, you'll find them here."

—Rick Bundschuh, author of <u>Incredible Questionnaires For Youth Ministry</u>

Purpose
Mr. Michael D. Williams, New York City
(permission granted)

Dear God,

I have yet to say good evening or good morning to you,
To compliment your creations, your sky, its shades of blue,
To thank you Lord for life and for seeing one more day,
For coming and going as I please, with nothing in my way.
I remember life as a child, Lord, scared of the terror by night,
You took that fear away from me, so now I walk upright.
But for reasons unknown, I am still afraid, for terror of a different kind.
Though I walk with both eyes open, I feel so hopelessly blind.
It's not a state of confusion Lord, because you have given me a peace of
*   mind.*
It's more of a longing for something that I have yet to find.
Lord, all I've ever wanted was to sing and make a video or two,
Then Jesus walked into my life and all my old turned new.
He gave me hope and faith to encourage those lost,
And motivated me towards righteousness at any cost.
But as I grew spiritually and people started to flock,
Instead of communing with Jesus, I sat proud in a lonely box
Wondering where did I go wrong, Lord, and what's with all the abuse.
But if you don't know one's purpose, there is bound to be some misuse.
So I'm coming to you, Lord, asking, is it something wrong in me?
And if so, could you please help because this man wants to be free.
Then I can be true to self and pure in heart.
Those were my best qualities.
Even when I was a mess, Lord, you saw fit to use me.
Souls were saved, lives were changed, miracles performed too,
All from the face of a scared little boy, just think what the man of God
*   can do.*
But I won't walk if you won't lead,
And I won't talk without your prophecy.
Lord, is it too much to ask you to finish what you have started in me?
I guess what I'm longing for is love, vision, hope, and peace,
All the things that will help me become the man that you want me to be.
I can feel the day approaching when I will stand boldly in your name,
Because the work you finished in me is perfect.
And I love you, Michael Dwayne.

A New Beginning
Rev. Ronnie A. Clark , Lynchburg, Virginia
(Printed by Permission)

A new beginning is a break with the past,
Not shackled and chained to yesterday,
But FREE at last.
A new beginning is a spiritual journey,
A pilgrimage to the Mecca within,
A place to renew our mind, body, and spirit,
For the NEW DAY beginning.
A new beginning is forgetting the pain and sad-
    ness of yesterday,
With its vain hopes and false dreams.
But yesterday made us who we are today
For we stand in the mirror of yesterday
Looking at ourselves today
Find strength, hope, and courage to conquer.
The NEWNESS of To-DAY
Only because we lived through yesterday.

Contents

INTRODUCTION

It seemed only a few days ago that the members of my class on a youth ministry walked through the door at Beulah Heights Bible College in Atlanta, Georgia. After spending hours preparing a syllabus for the fall semester 1996 class, suddenly it dawned on me: A text for this youth ministry class has already been chosen, but really it's only another book with just bits and pieces of information on ministering to youth. I'm Stuck! I am stuck with students, books, and a syllabus requiring students to complete an assignment to which I have never seen the answers.

The syllabus required students to write a paper on "How to Start a Youth Ministry," but I had not been able to find a single book which suggested a thorough step-by-step process, much less for teaching a class on this subject. I wondered how I should respond. Do I challenge my own teaching, or should I cancel the assignment altogether?

One problem in some youth ministries is the lack of structure. The lack of structure results from not considering the needed steps to start or modify a youth ministry and the lack of contents to meet the needs of students. This book will help the youth leader, youth workers, and those teaching youth ministry at Bible colleges and seminaries to know the steps and content for a youth ministry program.

After spending much time searching for a book on "How to Start a Youth Ministry," I had been informed by a major bookstore that no such book existed. I thought to myself, I realized that, in order for my students to write papers on "How to Start a Youth Ministry," I would have to teach the process myself. Though there are many books on youth ministry, steps for starting a youth ministry are not always visible. The question of how to start a youth ministry has always been puzzling.

Many leaders have been in the field of a youth ministry for years, but still do not know how to organize a youth ministry. Many teachers who instruct youth and youth leaders teach and lead poorly because they teach as leaders taught and led twenty years ago. Many of these leaders and teachers have taken their positions because they were placed there, not because they were called to this work. The African American church cannot afford to lose youth because of poor teachers and poor leaders. Church leaders and teachers instructing our young people must have a sincere desire to work with youth and to deal with their specific struggles.

One day I sat not in the pulpit, because of my choice, but in the congregation of the prominent Convent Avenue Baptist Church, New York City, November 30, 1997. I heeded the words of the pastor, Rev. Dr. Clarence Grant who spoke from Isaiah 11:1-5.

Like a branch that sprouts from a stump, someone from David's family will someday be king. The Spirit of the Lord will be with him to give him understanding, wisdom, and insight. He will be powerful, and he will know and honor the Lord. His greatest joy will be to obey the Lord. This king won't judge by appearances or listen to rumors. The poor and the needy will be treated with fairness and with justice. His word will be law everywhere in the land, and criminals will be put to death. Honesty and fairness will be his royal robes.

He made many interesting points, but one referred specifically to youth. Rev. Grant stated that many parents say their youth will not amount to anything and that saying harsh words degrades young people's morale and self-confidence. Many churches have already placed their youth in prison and have thrown away the key. Youth leaders have to beg for God's money because some finance teams and/or the deacon boards claim God's money as their personal funds and do not view youth ministry as a priority. Then, some pastors do not see the need to assist youth because of their own failures or bad youth experiences. Still other churches provide a bare minimum for the youth budget. Yet, the African American church wonders why youth are not in the church.

There are several reasons youth are not in the church. First, leaders do not have funds for activities and learning materials. Second, many older persons degrade youth because through the grace of God they have grown up and escaped some bad youth experiences of their own. Third, most churches do not have a curriculum to meet the needs of their youth. Youth today are going through a variety of difficult and harsh experiences. They need the grace of God and the church to be an example of what grace is all about.

Is there hope for the African American church youth? Yes, God is still providing grace and mercy. As Rev. Grant preached on November 30, 1997, God has still left the rod (the stump) that Isaiah discussed in chapter eleven of the Book of Isaiah. Although God could have taken roots of growth from Israel, He left a stump for new growth. The African American church must not stunt the growth of youth. God can still intervene and allow youth to return to the church. In fact, the stump already exists. It's a matter of whether your church will allow growth or destroy it!

Because of a lack of knowledge, many youth ministry programs consist of little more than a time for youth to meet and do their own thing. Both youth and leaders may just be simply hanging out or wasting time. Consequently, youth become bored and see no need to be part of the youth's ministry. The problem remains, of course, that no leader can predict exactly what repercussions being part of a youth ministry will have on how a young person learns and practices, but a seed cannot grow if it is never planted. The African American church must continue to plant and water more seeds in the fertile ground of our youth.

To plant a seed is to believe that all youth have a chance to survive and reach their greatest potential. To water the seed is to assist in the growth process. The church must be willing to provide more funds for a youth ministry and get rid of archaic views so youth can be the best Christians possible. This means that the church must take a second glance at activities and curriculum for the African American youth.

We should center activities on spirituality and spiritual growth, also include some fun activities that will motivate youth to attend youth meetings and church services. The teacher and the leader are the key persons for the development of our young people.

The youth leader is, naturally, responsible for what happens at youth meetings.

But, many leaders have few disciplinary skills and do not pay adequate attention to classroom order. Many leaders have little concern about classroom discipline because their own attitudes reflect "I don't care."

Having the right attitude is important when working with youth. A teacher with a nasty attitude should not be leading youth. Youth will quickly sense such an attitude and accept the negativity as a norm for classroom behavior and daily living. The youth leader is a key person for youth. When I reflect on my youth, I cannot recall any youth program.

Many youth ministers fall short of their task. Many leaders simply allow a youth ministry to be a time for meeting and discussing youth concerns. The main ingredient in any youth ministry program should be God's Word. Does your program allow time for teaching God's Word and does this take precedence over all other activities? It should.

Chapter One will address the question, "What is Youth Ministry?" Chapter Two will discuss Youth Workers." Chapter Three will describe "Twelve Suggested Steps for Starting a Youth Ministry." Chapter Four will provide "Suggestions For Youth Ministry Content." Chapter Five will present "Twenty-one Youth Discussion Topics." Chapter Six will provide "Twelve Youth Discussion Topics for Parents and Guardians."

CHAPTER ONE

What Is Youth Ministry?

What is a youth ministry? In **Investing in our African American Youth—You Can Handle It!** Darrell V. Freeman, Sr. informs readers that a youth ministry is "God working through the lives of Spirit-filled youth leaders to meet the holistic needs of young people" (13). In **What is Youth Ministry?** Mark Lamport suggests that a youth ministry should transform youth. He states:

> Youth ministry is the purposive, determined, and persistent quest by both natural and supernatural means to expose, transmit, or otherwise share with adolescents God's message of good news, which is central to the Christian faith. Its ultimate end is to cultivate a life transformation of youth by the power of the Holy Spirit that they might conform to the revealed Will of God as expressed in Scripture, and chiefly in the person of our Lord and Savior, Jesus Christ. (62)

In **Harper's Encyclopedia of Religious Education,** W. E. Barnick comments, "Youth ministry refers to all the activities of planning, support, and leadership within a religious community that are intended to engage and nurture youth in the outlook and priorities of that community" (712).

In **Working with Black Youth,** Charles Foster provides a purpose for black youth ministry. "The primary purpose for black youth ministry is to call youth into discipleship. This purpose embodies the identity and vocation central to the experence of adolescence. Identity has to do with allegiance and commitment—"Whose am I?" (103).

Youth ministry is one ministry that helps youth further discover the reality of being a Christian and the attributes needed to encourage others to fulfill their Christian duty. A youth ministry teaches youth to grow into adulthood using biblical principles for successful living, which also causes youth to find God's purpose in their lives.

Roland D. Martinson provides theological foundations and a definition for a youth ministry. Elaborating on youth ministry's message, mission and ministry, he states, "Youth ministry flows from the gospel message and mission as worship, witness, teaching, communion, and service" (26). The church must understand that her investment is not in vain.

Charles Nichols believes that youth ministry can be successful in various ways: "There is no one pattern for successful youth work" (152). Nichols gives three insightful ingredients: life-related theology, exemplary leadership, and goal-oriented programming (152). These three ingredients are needed for youth ministry. In addition, the cultural knowledge, understanding of youth development, and communication skills are also essential for a successful youth ministry.

CHAPTER TWO

Youth Workers

The youth worker should keep in mind the stages of youth. In "The Learner: Youth," **Introduction to Biblical Christian Education,** Charles Nichols states that youth are usually divided into two stages: early adolescence, ages twelve to fourteen, and middle adolescence, ages fifteen to seventeen (Nichols 147).

The qualifications for all youth workers should be carefully considered. Workers should not be recruited through announcements, fliers, or church bulletins, but should be recruited by church leaders after much praying. All workers should be observed concerning their attitudes, Christian behavior and their interest in youth. There is nothing worse than to have a youth worker who cannot understand the needs of youth, or to have a youth worker working with youth simply because no other person can be found. Meeting the needs of youth can be determined by an understanding of their stages of growth.

Youth workers should be sought through prayer. It is better not to advertise for someone to work with youth ministry. Many persons who answer an advertisement for employment have qualifications that match the job description, but the actual performance might not match the qualifications. In a ministry, we must remember that, just because someone looks good and has the qualifications, all of which are good, that person still might not enhance a ministry's program. Youth workers should be sought only after much praying and observation. A good youth worker is given by God rather than selected by people. The disciples selected the replacement for Judas. When God chooses persons, they are chosen in order to learn how to do the job. Perhaps the disciples concentrated so much on training a new leader that they forgot to ask God to select the new leader. There may be a person in your congregation to whom God has given ability to work with youth. But also consider whether that seemingly righteous person may be a murderer, a molester, or a drug dealer? How can you determine the godly man or woman? Simply by prayer. God never fails. God will send someone who is able do the task. We can only seek those who are in Christ. We all hope for the future, but only when Christians stay in the will of God, will Christians remain Christian.

The Christian youth worker should be a Christian who understands his or her theology, has a loving heart and an openness for youth, and believes that this work is a part of God's call in his or her life. The youth worker should also have leadership skills that include the ability to handle administration. The youth worker must understand that the group is comprised of youth. Doug Fields states, "For example, if you are working with a fourteen-year-old, allow him to act like a fourteen-year-old" (Fields 30). Many youth leaders want youth to act either like children or like adults. Youth leaders should realize that the work involves overseeing youth. Youth are distinct because they are at an age between adolescence and adult. They are shaping their future for adulthood. In a sense a youth worker is similar to a pastor. "Pastors oversee and attend to the needs of their people" (Fields 20).

The youth pastor or youth leader oversees the needs of youth. The pastor can assist the youth pastor or youth leader by encouraging youth to attend worship services.

If attendance in youth ministries is to increase, the pastor must stress attendance. The pastor should place emphasis upon increasing worship attendance. Len Kageler in his book, **How To Expand Your Youth Ministry—Practical Ways To Increase Your Attendance,** makes this point: when worship attendance is up, youth group attendance is up (15). In any case, God does the drawing of youth. Once a youth attends a meeting, the leader should consider what is needed in that person's life.

TWENTY-ONE SUGGESTIONS FOR YOUTH WORKERS

A youth worker should:

1. Be committed to the work
2. Be reminded that no one person knows everything
3. Be in constant prayer and Bible reading
4. Request others to keep you in prayer
5. Be organized
6. Be on time
7. Always seek new additional insights through training, attending workshops, etc.
8. Observe others from various settings in the church
9. Delete negative thoughts from the mind
10. Not gossip about the program and learners
11. Keep in mind his or her calling
12. Never forget the purpose of the ministry and the church's mission statement
13. Be peaceful in actions
14. Always think before acting
15. Know that it is better to resign than to remain unfaithful to youth
16. Understand how to teach youth using computers and Bible aids
17. Demonstrate youth ministry through music
18. Demonstrate youth ministry through tracts
19. Respect and hear the views of the youth minister
20. Respect and hear the views of the pastor and the Minister/Director of Christian Education
21. Possess skills for youth work

Workers should possess the following skills:

1. Know God
2. Have a Christian relationship with students and workers
3. Be committed to work (1 Timothy 4:10)
4. Be a model (1 Timothy 4:12)
5. Desire to work with youth
6. Communicate the truth (1 Timothy 4:13)

QUALIFICATIONS FOR THE YOUTH LEADER

All Christian job descriptions should state what the worker is expected to do.

Biblical Job Description

1. Guard the flock. Acts 20:28

   Look after yourselves and everyone the Spirit has placed in your care. Be like shepherds to God's church. It is the flock that he bought with the blood of his own Son.

2. Oversee the flock. Acts 20:28

   Look after yourselves and everyone the Holy Spirit has placed in your care. Be like shepherds to God's church. It is the flock that he bought with the blood of his own Son.

3. Agonize over the flock. Acts 20:31

   Be on your guard! Remember how day and night for three years I kept warning you with tears in my eyes.

4. Know the flock. John 10:3

   The sheep know their shepherd's voice. He calls each of them by name and leads them out.

5. Equip the flock. Colossians 1:28

   We announce the message about Christ, and we use all our wisdom to warn and teach everyone, so that all of Christ's followers will grow and become mature.

6. Reprove, rebuke, and exhort the flock. 2 Timothy 4:2

   To preach God's message. Do it willingly, even if it isn't the popular thing to do. You must correct people and point out their sins. But also cheer them up, and when you instruct them, always be patient.

7. Tenderly love the flock. 1 Thessalonians 2:7

   But as apostles, we could have demanded help from you. After all, Christ is the one who sent us. We chose to be like children or like a mother nursing her baby.

8. Evangelize the world. 2 Timothy 4:5

   But you must stay calm and be willing to suffer. You must work hard to tell the good news and to do your job well.

9. Endure severe reactions. 2 Timothy 4:3

The time is coming when people won't listen to good teaching. Instead, they will look for teachers who will please them by telling them only what they are itching to hear.

10. Feed the Flock. Acts 20:28

Dewey Bertolini takes the above ten steps in the chart from **Back To The Heart Of Youth,** Copyright (c) 1984. Used by Permission of Dewey M. Bertolini (29).

All workers should consider the following quoted Scriptures.

IMPORTANCE OF TEACHING GOD'S WORD

1 Timothy 4:6:

If you teach these things to other followers, you will be a good servant of Christ Jesus. You will show that you have grown up on the teachings about our faith and on the good instructions you have obeyed.

1 Timothy 4:7a:

Don't have anything to do with worthless, senseless stories.

1 Timothy 4:7b-9:

Work hard to be truly religious. As the saying goes, "Exercise is good for your body, but religion helps you in every way. It promises life now and forever." These words are worthwhile and should not be forgotten.

2 Chronicles 16:9:

The Lord is constantly watching everyone, and he gives strength to those who faithfully obey him. But you have done a foolish thing, and your kingdom will never be at peace again.

NEED FOR SPIRITUAL CLEANSING

Isaiah 1:16-17:

Wash yourselves clean! I am disgusted with your filthy deeds. Stop doing wrong and learn to live right. See that justice is done. Defend widows and orphans and help those in need.

2 Timothy 2:19, 21:

> But the foundation that God has laid is solid. On it is written, "The Lord knows who his people are. So everyone who worships the Lord must turn away from evil." That's also how it is with people. The ones who stop doing evil and make themselves pure will become special. Their lives will be holy and pleasing to their Master, and they will be able to do all kinds of good deeds.

1 Samuel 13:13-14:

> "That was stupid!" Samuel said. "You didn't obey the Lord your God. If you had obeyed him, someone from your family would always have been king of Israel. But no, you disobeyed, and so the Lord won't choose anyone else from your family to be king. In fact, he has already chosen the one he wants to be the next leader of his people."

GOD'S ANGER AGAINST THOSE WHO REFUSE TO FOLLOW HIS WAYS

Numbers 20:12:

> But the Lord said to Moses and Aaron, "Because you refused to believe in my power, these people did not respect me. And so, you will not be the ones to lead them into the land I have promised."

2 Samuel 6:7:

> The Lord God was very angry at Uzzah for doing this, and he killed Uzzah right there beside the chest.

The leader should make sure that all workers understand to whom they should report. They should understand salaries, how much time is required for the ministry, meeting times, do's and don'ts, lines of authority, and consequences for breaking guidelines for both leaders and youth. Youth meeting rules should be understood by both youth and leaders. Rules should be developed by the entire team: youth and youth leaders alike.

CHAPTER THREE

Twelve Suggested Steps For Starting A Youth Ministry

TWELVE SUGGESTED STEPS FOR STARTING A YOUTH MINISTRY

1. Decide on the staf
2. Select a youth leader
3. Determine a location for the youth ministry
4. Look at congregational or community history
5. Look at the vision of the leader or the community
6. Decide on the name of the ministry
7. Identify the age group with which one will minister
8. Study other youth ministry programs of similar age group or the same culture
9. Discuss goals, objectives, lesson planning, and general planning
10. Decide on the opening event
11. Decide on staff meeting date
12. Decide on content for the youth ministry program

Step One—Decide on the Staff

The youth staff should consist of a team who is loving to each other and to youth. It is very important for youth leaders to show a Christlike loving spirit. Many youth leaders come and go because they are not committed to the work. A youth worker must sense a call and desire to do this kind of work.

Step Two—Selecting a Youth Leader

When thinking about selecting a leader, one should ask whether or not the leader knows God. Does the leader talk about praying, reading the Word of God daily and weekly, and walking with God daily and weekly? Many Christians have been taught the need to stay in touch with God. It is important to seek spiritual growth before being in a responsible position for youth. In addition to knowing God, youth workers should have some interpersonal skills, be committed to the task, be a model, have a desire to work with youth, and be able to communicate the truth.

Interpersonal skills are very much needed for youth leaders. These skills should include: being committed to the job, acting as a role model, being able to communicate the truth, viewing the ministry as a gift, maturing and developing Christian relationships with students and team members.

In the article "What are the Necessary Competencies to be an Effective Youth Worker?" Rick Dunn discusses interpersonal effectiveness. He says that interpersonal effectiveness can be defined as "one's ability to develop meaningful interpersonal ministry relationships which increasingly 'image' God's love" (30). The youth leader should be a caring individual, mirroring the way that God cares for everyone. To teach or preach the Gospel involves meeting youth where they are.

Being **committed to the task** is very important for the youth leader. A leader who is not committed to the job might use the youth ministry for personal gain. The ministry is for the glory of God, not for self-gain.

Modeling is very important. Talking "Christian" is easy, but are you honestly trying to improve your spiritual journey? Are you an example of what others should follow? It is important to be a Christian model to those we serve. Many are not where they desire to be spiritually, but we all can improve our spiritual well-being. Being an example means living so that others do not have to hear your title, but can look at your life and automatically see who you are. Being an example is presenting oneself as a Christian model for others to follow.

A youth leader should **have a desire to work with youth.** God calls everyone to a particular ministry. The person obeys the will of God and makes the experience an enjoyable one. If someone does not like his or her job, that person might not be an effective leader. If you are called to work with a certain group, such as youth, you might consider the varying youth ages. Unless God has specified the age, select the age that interests you.

Above all else, the youth leader should possess the skill to **communicate the truth.** The Word of God must be conveyed to youth. To communicate the truth, you need to know the truth. You know the truth through study of God's Word.

Step Three—Location for the Youth Ministry

The location where the youth ministry is to be held is very important to the leader. Will the ministry take place in a church? If the ministry is not in a church, does the community have a sufficient youth population? Remember, there should be youth in the area of the youth ministry site. This is not mandatory but might prove to be helpful in the future. What about transportation? Can youth ride a bus, walk, or find other ways to attend the ministry?

Step Four—Congregational and Community History

Knowledge of the history of the congregation or community is very important for developing a youth ministry. If a history is available, use it. If not, church leaders may begin compiling and keeping its church history in a safe place. A committee could be formed to research the history. The history should be made available to the congregation. The history should inform the leader about the church's actual history and specifically about youth work. Hopefully, names of past and current youth workers will be a part of the history, giving the leader an opportunity to contact former leaders.

The congregational history will also share the progression of the church. The new youth leader should keep in mind that new ideas are not easily understood. Provide an overview of the vision rather than present ideas at once. Congregational history can provide some insights about needed changes for a youth ministry. The congregational history should include history of the youth at a church. If youth history is not included in the congregational history, a youth leader may elect a committee to interview former and present youth leaders.

If there is no church building or location for the youth ministry, the church or community can also play a very important role in the organization of the youth ministry. Community history will inform the leader about buildings or areas where youth met. For example, a survey of the community might ask questions about the needs that youth have. In addition, once the community sees the seriousness of the intent of the youth leader, some members of the community might show active concern in developing a new program. The concerns might be financial aid or hands on help.

Someone who is familiar with writing history should assist in writing community history. The history should be written after facts have been collected. The population of the community, as well as the makeup of the community may be included. This data, after careful scrutiny, will inform a leader of local youth's needs. Remember that a youth ministry is formed to help youth with both physical and spiritual needs. God cares for the "whole" youth.

Step Five—Vision of the Leader or the Community

Prior to considering the vision of the leader or community, you should consider the nature of the ministry. Jesus Christ announced His beginning ministry and its nature in Luke 4:18-19:

> The Lord's Spirit has come to me, because he has chosen me to tell the good news to the poor. The Lord has sent me to announce freedom for prisoners, to give sight to the blind, to free everyone who suffers.

The pastor's vision is very important in a youth ministry. The church should acknowledge the pastor as the called person to lead the congregation. The role of the pastor will vary from denomination to denomination. By all means, seek your denomination's handbook before making a decision regarding the role of your pastor or the one under whom you are to work. A youth ministry is only one component of the church. The pastor should have the first and last word about the ministry. All approvals should come from the minister of Christian education. The pastor serves as the contact person when the minister of Christian education is not available.

The youth minister should regularly schedule meetings with the minister of Christian education to discuss youth ministry. It is wise to have everything in writing. For example, if the minister of Christian education approves a field trip, have him or her provide permission in writing. Should the minister of Christian education forgets (and with heavy workloads, it could happen) that permission was granted, permission will be valid.

In the case of the secular community, the vision of the secular community should be kept in mind in planning the youth ministry. The youth leader must hear the vision of the faith community and teach faith principles to youth, but at the same time, the leader must understand secular community actions and study their views without robbing the secular community of its culture. When the youth leader acknowledges the vision of the secular community, the youth leader will understand his or her goals for the ministry. When the community has no collective vision, the youth leader may be looked upon to suggest goals for the community.

*RESOURCE

"Refuges from Racism: Adolescent Community Settings As An Early Motivational Influence for High Achieving Black Men: A Theoretical Perspective." Ph.D. Thesis, City University Graduate Center, 1998.

Step Six—Decide on the Name of the Ministry

If a name has already been established for the ministry, then maintain that name. However, if you consider a name for the ministry, why not allow the youth to suggest names. Then have youth to vote by ballot at the next meeting for the name of the ministry. Youth will work harder when they can feel ownership of youth ministry.

Step Seven—Identify the Age Group With Which You Will Minister

What age will you work with? Will you work with ages 12-14, ages 13-16, ages 16-18, ages 18-21, and so on? The age group should be determined in advance for planning an effective youth ministry. All teaching materials, activities, and events should relate to the selected age group. You may divide youth according to grades; for example; junior high or senior high. This is really a matter of individual choice. What works best in one setting may or may not work in another setting.

Step Eight—Study Other Ministry Programs of Similar Age Group or Culture

Studying other ministries might be helpful to a new ministry. Do not attempt to use everything that you hear, see, or read. Use suggestions that are most beneficial to your ministry. When glancing at other ministries, the following questions might be kept in mind:

1. How do they recruit youth for their ministry?
2. How did their ministry get started?
3. Can they share any budget suggestions?
4. What is their planning process?
5. How often does their youth group meet?
6. How many workers assist the leader in the ministry?
7. What are some positive and negative aspects of a youth ministry?
8. Who determines the agenda for youth meetings?
9. How much time does the leader spend teaching the Word of God to youth?
10. Is there any other advice that this ministry could provide to someone starting a youth ministry?

Step Nine—Discuss Goals, Objectives, Lesson Planning and General Planning

The goals and objectives will be your road maps to success. Leaders need to reflect the vision of both the pastor and the secular community and then create goals and objectives for the youth ministry. Goals and objectives should keep in mind the survey results from youth. All youth should be given the opportunity to participate in completing survey questions. The survey should be completed voluntarily with no signed names.

In developing a program, a committee should be in place to help with developing and distributing the questionnaire. The same or a different committee may develop goals and objectives. If church workers are going to work with you in starting a youth ministry in the community, all workers should be part of your organizational meeting. Make sure the workers are all called to a youth ministry and that the team agrees with your vision, goals, and objectives.

Goals:

Goals are general views. Goals are the overall big picture.

Decide on what you intend to accomplish in your youth ministry program.

* See Appendix—Form One

Objectives:

Objectives are specifics. Objectives are written from the goals. Objectives are short steps toward the goal. Decide on three or more objectives for each goal. For further explanations or examples, see appendix—Form Two.

Lesson Planning:

The leader should decide on lesson plans to meet the objectives. The leader should review all lesson plans before they are taught. Deadlines are important for teachers. Do not worry about the number of youth present for a lesson; plan for one as you would plan for fifty. Planning time is needed for workers. Leaders may consider team planning. The ministry does not belong to one leader. Everybody plays a role: parents, youth, the congregation, the pastor, the minister of Christian education, and the youth minister. The leader should determine the actual lesson plan design.

RESOURCE

Barna, George. <u>Generation Next.</u> Ventura, California: Regal Books, 1995.

General Planning:

You may plan quarterly, semiannually or annually. Start to plan semiannually because time quickly passes for the next planning session. The planning session should consist of all workers and at least two youth. The leader should inform the attendees that they are to provide the floor plans, but the actual construction might slightly alter, if the leader envisions changes. The leader may make suggestions after the committee provides a plan or proposal. The leader should submit the plan to the minister of Christian education or the director of Christian education. The leader can then insert some ideas for changes that might better the ministry. This committee should meet at least twice during the first six months. Each session might last from two to five half-days. Sessions might be held over a period of two to three weeks. In addition, planning is needed for review and changes of the original plan. The agenda should be very clear. Refreshments should be served; breakfast or dinner should also be provided to show appreciation for those attending.

The final plan can be implemented as the youth leader suggests. In any case, a review of plans is needed. The minister of Christian education or the director of Christian education may revise the plan. Much planning should occur.

Step Ten—Decide on the Opening Event

The opening event for a youth ministry is crucial to the ministry's success. This event can encourage youth to attend the meeting or the event can discourage youth to attend. Carefully plan the opening event. Remember the first impression is usually the lasting one. Make a good impression. Think about the location, the size of the group anticipated, the refreshments, the activities and the opening message that you want to convey. Do not overdo this session. You cannot accomplish everything at one meeting. Announce at this meeting the youth schedule for future meetings. A successful opening event is when directions have been clear and youth understand the objectives for ministry.

Step Eleven—Decide on Staff Meeting Dates

The staff should know meeting times far in advance. Staff meetings for the year should be a part of the youth ministry calendar. The leader of the staff should remember that most people are volunteers and that people have other responsibilities. The length of each meeting should be kept at a minimum. When you meet more than one hour, thoughts become fuzzy. If the meeting is scheduled for half-days, make sure that a break is given at each hour. Upon returning to the meeting, something fun should be done for about five minutes. This may be a game or something that will spark interest for the group.

Step Twelve—Content for the Youth Ministry Program

Deciding on content is not easy. Both learning activities and general activities are needed. Learning activities are those activities that accompany a lesson. They attempt to provide an opening, sum up a point or close a lesson. The activity is centered around the content of the lesson and is another way for the lesson to be better understood. General activities, however, are for fun. They may include going bowling, skating, basketball, and similar events. Such activities are needed, but they should not be the core of the program. The Word of God must be the heart and foundation for every youth ministry program.

Because God is the foundation, youth programs must teach biblical insights. They should help youth and their parents better understand the relationship that youth have with both society and the church. Yet, more particularly, what is needed for the African American Youth?

The African American church should consider three questions:

1. What problems exist in our African American youth community?
2. How can the African American church youth program help the African American youth overcome the problems that beset them?
3. What should the African American youth already involved in a youth ministry do to help other African American Youth not connected to a youth ministry or church?

Because of the severity of these questions, we will continue their discussion in the next chapter.

CHAPTER FOUR

Suggestions for Youth Ministry Content

The African American youth ministry program has similar components to non-African American youth ministries. The major difference is culture. An African American youth should be taught how to cope with his or her particular culture-related problems, i.e., drugs, police brutality, low employment, and academic difficulties. All youth ministries should be centered around God. The African American church youth program is unique because it teaches how God is at work in the African American community. The African American youth program teaches African American heritage, i.e., biblical heritage and African American culture. The African American youth program should include teaching African heritage.

Content for the African American youth program is very important to youth and their families. Content should be decided upon after trying the following ideas:

(1) Glancing at the twelve steps,

(2) Using some form of survey questions, such as the ones included in the appendix, and

(3) Spending much time in prayer, fasting and reading God's Word.

Content in the youth's program can cause harm if not carefully sought and planned. There are many good resources. The Bible is the main resource for a youth ministry. Leaders and teachers must not forget that they should not give their interpretation of Scripture unless they feel led by the Spirit. If you don't know what the Word is saying, ask another person who might have more knowledge than you do to help clear up questions. Do not simply select content because it sounds good, or because others are using it; select content that will serve your setting, and will be consistent with that which is to be accomplished.

Sample Questions To Answer When Deciding On Content For Your Youth Ministry Program

1. What problems exist in the African American community in which you live?
2. What content should be included in your African American church youth program?
3. What should African American youth already involved in a youth ministry do to help other African American youth not connected to a youth ministry or church?

Question one: What problems exist in the African American youth community in which you live?

There is a long list of problems among African American youth that goes on and on. Familiar things such as drugs, illicit sex, gangs, and violence, but really all the problems add up to one major problem, breaking strongholds. Strongholds will be discussed under **Lock Two: Self-Esteem.**

RESOURCES
Community boards, local elected officials, studies on youth conducted by your state.

Question two: What content should be included in the youth program?

Three locks and twelve keys serve as a starting point for developing the African American youth program. Locks are themes for discussion. Keys are subtopics. Themes may be short or long-term. Youth leaders should attempt to teach the following three locks and twelve keys in youth ministry.

Content for Your
Youth Ministry Program

Three Locks

Twelve Keys

1. The entire Word of God
2. Prayer
3. Understanding Christian theology
4. Biblical principles
5. Knowing how to learn and distinguish spiritual gifts
6. Teach the meaning of Christian worship
7. Know how to evangelize
8. Understanding how to deal with strongholds
9. Decisions that affect the whole person
10. Understanding purpose
11. Teaching how to love God, self and others
12. Teaching twelve sticky subjects
    a. Marriage
    b. Divorce
    c. Death/dying
    d. Various cultures
    e. African history
    f. African roots in Scripture
    g. Male/female
    h. Sexuality
    i. Drugs/alcohol
    j. Peer pressure
    k. Parenting
    l. Planning for life

Lock One—The Bible

The first and most important lock in any youth ministry is teaching the Word of God. Too many youth programs are made up of fun activities only. It is okay to have fun, but only after the Word of God has been taught. The primary purpose of every youth ministry is to teach the Word of God. After youth hear the Word of God, they should allow the Word to speak to them in such a way that each person's purpose in life will be found.

RESOURCES

The Contemporary English Bible, The New King James Bible

Lock Two—Self-Esteem

The second lock for any youth ministry is teaching self-esteem. Self-esteem is a lock that every youth ministry should consider. Self-esteem is a belief in self, to be worthy or successful. In **Preaching For Black Self-Esteem,** the authors, Henry Mitchell and Emil Thomas, discuss ethnic self-esteem. "In short, self -esteem is a personal judgment of worthiness that is expressed in the attitudes the individual holds toward himself" (4-5). Leaders should be reminded about ethnic self-esteem. The youth ministry program should assist youth in defining their identity. Working with youth over the past twenty years, I have observed that youth need a lot of work in the area of self-esteem. Many youth come from broken homes, no home, or a home where self-esteem is not taught. Jim Burns, author of **The Youth Builder,** writes about the primary task of teens: "The primary task of the preteen and teenager is to construct a self-identity" (Burns 34).

RESOURCES
Bevere, John. Breaking Intimidation—How to Overcome Fear and Release the Gifts of God in Your Life. Orlando, Florida. Creation House, 1995.
Coopersmith, Stanley. The Antecedents of Self-Esteem. San Francisco: W. H. Freeman and Company, 1967.
Jackson, Chris. Straight Talk on Tough Topics. Grand Rapids. Zondervan Publishing House, 1996.
Mitchell, Henry H. and Emil Thomas. Preaching for Black Self-Esteem. Nashville. Abingdon Press, 1994.

Lock Three—Self Values

A third lock is teaching self values. The leader should carefully consider this area, which indeed covers much territory. First, many youth need to deal with injustice. Youth must be taught that God has given us the power to overcome things that beset us in life. The best way to fight social injustice is to have Christ in your life. This does not exclude standing up for one's rights. Having Christ in your life means that when you speak, Christ will speak through you. The church must teach Christ. Youth ministry should teach youth right from wrong. In **Don't Check Your Brains at the Door,** Josh McDowell and Bob Hostetler tell how easy it is to know right from wrong when they write, "The amazing thing is that you don't need a Ph.D. to distinguish right from wrong. A Christian youth leader should know right from wrong" (McDowell and Hostetler 93).

Key 1—The Entire Word Of God

The version of the Bible which your ministry will use should be carefully selected. Some versions of the Bible might not clearly provide a description of the Word of God. The entire Word should be taught. Leaders should begin where students are. For example, some students are not ready for the Book of Revelation at the beginning, nor is it important to start with Genesis and teach books in any consecutive order. Subjects should include Salvation and the Holy Spirit. The Word of God provides power for believers.

Luke 10:19-20 states:

> *I have given you the power to trample on snakes and scorpions and to defeat the power of your enemy Satan. Nothing can harm you. But don't be happy because evil spirits obey you. Be happy that your names are written in heaven.*

John 4:4 states:

> *Children, you belong to God, and you have defeated these enemies. God's Spirit is in you and more powerful than the one that is in the world.*

Mark 16:18:

> *They will handle snakes and will drink poison and not be hurt. They will also heal sick people by placing their hands on them.*

Matthew 18:18

> *I promise you that God in heaven will allow whatever you allow on earth, but he will not allow anything you don't allow.*

Then one cannot help but read...

> *2 Timothy 1: 7- God's Spirit doesn't make cowards out of us. The Spirit gives us power, love, and self-control.*

RECOMMENDED RESOURCE

A Bible version such as the Revised King James Version. A paraphrased version may not help students understand the translated Word of God. If a paraphrased version is used, students should understand that the version includes statements in which the author might use in his or her own speech.

Key 2—Prayer

After teaching a course on prayer at a Bible college, it was discovered that many lay and ordained ministers knew very little about prayer. Many people only know that prayer is the key to heaven and that faith unlocks the door. Many times we assume that anyone in a Christian setting knows about prayer. But we must ask: Are we really teaching the meaning of prayer? For example, I ask students if God ever changes His mind. Most students reply, "No." The truth is that God changed His mind on various occasions because the righteous person prayed and trusted and petitioned God. God could destroy many people but in many cases, prayers encourage Him to change His mind, but never His will. God becomes angry on a number of occasions, but the prayers of the righteous availeth, and God's anger is assuaged.

The youth ministry program should devote itself to teach youth how to pray, explore the meaning of prayer, and offer direction about how to seek God.

RESOURCES

Glover, C. E. <u>A Training Manual for Establishing A Prayer Ministry in the African-American Church—The Missing Link—Prayer.</u> Plantation, Florida, LCA Publications, 1996. (Pastor Mount Bethel Baptist Church, Fort Lauderdale, Florida).

Hunt, T. <u>The Doctrine of Prayer.</u> Nashville: Convention Press, 1986.

MacArthur, John, Jr. <u>Jesus' Pattern of Prayer.</u> Chicago: The Moody Bible Institute, 1981.

Samolyk, Janet, <u>There is a Reason to Pray,</u> Morris Publishers, 1996.

Key 3—Christian Theology

In **Restoring At-Risk Communities: Doing It Together And Doing It Right,** John M. Perkins discusses some major points for Christian education. He speaks of having a spiritual relationship with God, how to love one another, how to respect one another, learning the Christian duty, and understanding the role of the church, to name a few of his points. Most strikingly were his key elements in a theology of the Christian community. The youth ministry program should teach youth about Christian theology. Nothing is more important than understanding what the Christian should believe and understand.

Every leader should read and become familiar with these elements when developing content for youth ministry.

The key elements in "A Theology Of Christian Community Development" are found in John Perkins' book, **Restoring At-Risk Communities** (c) 1995. Used by permission.

The Key Elements in a Theology of Christian Community Development

* The Christian community development approach to the problem of community development is based on 'time-tested' biblical principles
* Mankind's deepest needs are for a spiritual relationship with God. In Christian community development, the local church is the most effective agent in bringing about that relationship
* The biblical vision for Christian community development is for people to be in loving fellowship with God and with one another as they toil in fruitful labor, which benefits their community of need. The family as a unit must be reinforced. Leadership for their needed common efforts comes from within their own community
* The methodology of Christian community development—relocation, reconciliation, and redistribution—is merely a restatement, in man-made terms, of clear biblical principles
* God's master plan of reconciliation is to bring all things in heaven and earth under one head. If the gospel is not concerned with reconciling us across the most stubborn ethnic and racial barriers, then it is no gospel at all

* When viewed from the Bible, the Christian community development principle of redistribution has three parts to it: everything belongs to God; God said 'there should be no poor among you,' and provided law, which allowed the poor to reclaim their portion of his wealth; and God makes us wealthy so that we can reinvest in His work
* The clearest example of the principle of relocation in the Bible is that of Christ's act of love for us in leaving heaven to come to earth and, once here, giving His life for us
* The wheel of ministry provides a helpful model for understanding the biblical concept of salvation. The wheel's components are call, evangelism, social action, economic development, and justice, with the church at the center (Perkins 45-46).

The youth program must teach youth how to deal with and how to destroy strongholds. Seminars, discussions, and curriculum must include teaching time on strongholds.

RESOURCES

Cone, James H. A Black Theology of Liberation. Mary Knoll, New York: Obis Books, 1989.

King, Robert and Peter C. Hodgson, editors. Christian Theology. Minneapolis: Fortress Press, 1982.

Perkins, John. Restoring At-Risk Communities—Doing it Together and Doing it Right. Grand Rapids: Baker Book House Company, 1995.

Key 4—Biblical Principles

There are biblical principles for living. The youth should get a clear picture of what God requires of us. Many times people sin because they do not know that it is a violation of God's Word. When the principles are taught, one might live a better life. A good place to start is the Ten Commandments.

RESOURCE: The Bible

Key 5—How To Learn And Distinguish Spiritual Gifts

There are many books on spiritual gifts. Spiritual gifts are gifts that Christians are given from God (see 1 Corinthians

12:1-12). In **Discover Your Gifts And Learn How To Use Them,** Alvin J. Vander Griend states "Spiritual gifts are special abilities given by Christ through the Holy Spirit to empower believers for the ministries of the body (15). Spiritual gifts are given to help Christians minister to one another. Observe Paul in 1 Corinthians 12:7 that gifts are for the common good and Peter in 1 Peter 4:10 who suggests that our gifts are to serve others. Spiritual gifts are also given to build up the Body of Christ (Ephesians 4:11-16), and to Glorify God (1 Peter 4:11) (Griend 15).

Teach students the spiritual gifts and how to keep the gifts. Many people lose their gifts through disobedience to God. It is easy to slip and lose that with which God has blessed you. Use your gifts, and teach youth to use their gift(s). Youth in turn can teach others about how to identify and use their gifts in service to God and others.

Teaching African American youth about spiritual gifts helps their self-esteem. Such teaching demonstrates to them that they are already "good" at something that God has given them.

RECOMMENDED RESOURCE
Griend, Alvin. <u>Discover Your Gifts And Learn How To Use Them.</u>
   Grand Rapids: CRC Publications, 1996.

Scriptures To Consider On Spiritual Gifts:

1 Timothy 4:14; 2 Timothy 1:6; Exodus 35:31; Romans 12:8, 1 Corinthians 12; Romans 12: 5-6; Ephesians 4: 8-12, to name a few.

Key 6—Teach The Meaning Of Christian Worship
   It is assumed that youth know about worship. I have experienced youth worship and senior worship at all levels. Youth worship should lead youth to better understand senior worship services. In my observations, I am not sure if some churches comprehend the true meaning of youth worship. All leaders of the church must plan youth worship.

Youth should be taught not only how to read Scripture, but how to seek God and understand the Word of God. Churches must place emphasis upon the Word and not the preacher. Maybe some youth see the preacher as the head of the church, but when the preacher makes a mistake, those youth become hurt or leave the church. The youth should see God in the preacher and, regardless of the person delivering the message, hear the Word of God. This is not an allowance for the preacher to do what he desires, but one should understand that even the preacher is imperfect. A church having problems with any leader should have counsel with the leader, pray for the leader, and unless a serious crime, allow the leader to continue working and at the same time, improve his or her character. Many times seeking professional help should be recommended.

The youth program should prepare your youth for worship. Teach youth how to read Scripture, how to act in church and how to hear and listen for key words in the sermon. Most of all, teach youth the need to have and read a Bible in church services.

People need the right relationship with God. If people learn how to worship God, blessings will come down. Sickness, diseases, and worldly problems might disappear when we learn how to worship God. God must be seen in Scripture in spite of our conditions. The Word of God gives us assurance that God will do it for us.

Key 7—How To Evangelize

Many times the youth program does not teach anything about evangelizing. Evangelizing is spreading the Gospel. Even though many publishing companies teach evangelizing, teachers still teach edification. Edification is improving our morality by lifting up the name of our Lord. The African American church must move to write its own literature not simply to include edification, but also evangelism. The youth program should teach youth how to evangelize.

RECOMMENDED RESOURCES

Towns, Elmer. Your Ministry of Evangelism—A Guide for Church Volunteers. Wheaton: Evangelical Training Association, 1991.

Urban Ministries. Black Evangelism: Which Way from Here. Kansas City: Nazarene Publishing House, 1974.

Key 8—How To Deal With Strongholds

What is a Stronghold? In **Breaking Strongholds in the African-American Family: Strategies for Spiritual Warfare,** Dr. Clarence Walker states:

> *Anything that opposes Christ is from His enemy, the devil; thus strongholds are from Satan and his demonic host. They (strongholds) must be destroyed, brought down, obliterated, and demolished. (14)*

A Stronghold is that grip on one's life that keeps him or her from reaching God's spiritual heights. Some Scriptures helpful in understanding this concept are provided.

2 Corinthians 10:3-5

> *We live in this world, but we don't act like its people or fight our battles with the weapons of this world. Instead, we use God's power that can destroy fortresses. We destroy arguments and every bit of pride that keeps anyone from knowing God. We capture people's thoughts and make them obey Christ.*

Proverbs 18:19

> *Making up with a friend you have offended is harder than breaking through a city wall.*

Ephesians 6:12

> *We are not fighting against humans. We are fighting against forces and authorities and against rulers of darkness and powers in the spiritual world.*

Exodus 20:5

> *Don't bow down and worship idols. I am the LORD your God, and I demand all your love. If you reject me, I will punish your families for three or four generations.*

Ezekiel 16:44

> *People will use this saying about you, Jerusalem: 'If the mother is bad, so is her daughter.'*

After reading Dr. Clarence Walker's Book, **Breaking Strongholds In The African-American Family: Strategies For Spiritual Warfare,** I agree with the author that the African American family must realize that our African American men, women, youth, and children, all come under the umbrella of the African American Family. The family relationship might not be what one would desire, but those you hang with and those you live with are really your family. Sad to say, many African Americans have formed a new family because their blood family does not exist or does not care to be bothered with them. In any case, the family nucleus exists. Dr. Walker discusses foundational strongholds: Fear, Anger, and Idolatry. Then he discusses strongholds among men, women, and youth.

The author also speaks to men about some strongholds. For example, he states that some men might have:

1. The fear of intimacy syndrome (lack of attention and affection)
2. The bloody warrior syndrome (anger)
3. The nimrod syndrome (pride)
4. The neo-polygamous sexuality (having more than one mate at a time)

(Walker 27-34).

Women might have the following strongholds:

1. The Jezebel Syndrome (a quest for power, control, and predominance of her religious ideas)
2. The Cutting Tongue (talking)
3. The Codependency (must have relationship with the same type of person, i.e., alcoholics seek alcoholics)
4. The Tamar Complex (reflects the assault or rape)

(Walker 35-41).

The author then discusses four strongholds in youth:

1. The Tribalism Syndrome (one group against another; youth take part in a certain group in order to form tribal relatives)

2. Out-of-Wedlock Deadlock (sex before marriage)
3. Negative Music (music that does not magnify Christ)
4. Low Self-Esteem (Black self-hate)
(Walker 43-46).

The above three groups: men, women, and youth are important categories to understand. Men, women and youth have the tendency to take on each other's syndromes or what I call the Carry Over Syndrome. If Satan cannot involve an individual in one area, he will surely attempt to involve one in another area. All syndromes create a stronghold against the family. The church should then consider all problems in the youth's community, not as problems, but as strongholds. When the youth ministry considers strongholds, one can begin to teach youth how God can destroy strongholds among their friends and family. Teaching one member of the family how to overcome strongholds will help the entire family to become aware of strongholds.

Strongholds are taken from the book: **Breaking Strongholds In The African-American Family** by Dr. Clarence Walker. Copyright (c)1966 by Dr. Clarence Walker. Used by permission of Zondervan Publishing House.

RESOURCES
Bernal, Dick. Curses—What They are and How to Break Them. San Jose: California, Jubilee Christian Center, 1996.
Pearson, Carlton. Breaking the Curse—The Ultimate Act of Devotion. Write for books and video, Carlton Pearson Ministries: Higher Dimensions Family Bookstore, 8621 S. Memorial Drive, Tulsa, Ok 74133 1-877 HIGHERD
Sumrall, Lester. 101 Questions and Answers on Demon Powers. Tulsa: Harrison House, 1983.

Key 9—Decisions That Affect The Whole Person
Making decisions is not always easy. The youth should be taught how to make the right decisions. Youth are prone to conform with the crowd or group. Youth must be taught how to say no. Many youth are afraid to say no because of circumstances, such as being a member of gangs. The youth

ministry should develop a program to help youth withdraw from gangs. When Christian youth become a part of gangs, the youth ministry program should provide youth with information about gang life. Many youth seek gangs for friendship. In any crowd or groups, teaching friendship is important to youth.

Youth should be taught how to select friends and the meaning of friendship. Real friendship can only take place when one is a friend to God. In other words, having a friendship relationship with God is the beginning of understanding and true friendship.

Economic development should teach youth how to pool resources in order to survive in this world. The youth should meet business leaders and be exposed to job careers at an early age.

The youth program should invite speakers to deal with the subjects. Many youth become the victims of crime because they often take the wrong action. The youth program should teach youth how to deal with the whole person.

RECOMMENDED RESOURCES

Dobson, James. Life on the Edge. Nashville: Word Publishers, 1995.
Wimberly, Edward P. African-American Pastoral Care. Nashville: Abingdon Press, 1991.

Key 10—Understanding Purpose

Youth must be taught that their primary purpose is to serve others. How to serve others must be taught. The youth leader must then teach youth about the destination, vision, and how to exercise their vision and values.

RESOURCES

Barnes, Edward J. The Black Community As The Source Of Positive Self-Concept for Black Children: A Theoretical Perspective, "Social Problems" 43 (3), 107-123.
Coles, Robert. How to Raise a Moral Child—The Moral Intelligence of Children. New York: Random House, 1997.
Spurlock, J. Development of Self-Concept in Afro-American Children, "Hospital and Community Psychology" 37, 66-70.
Whitt, Jim and Sondra. Road Signs for Success. 1-800-874-4928.

Key 11—Teaching How To Love God, Self, And Others

Many Christians do not love themselves. They degrade themselves when they should be caring and nurturing themselves. When a youth is taught how to love God, then the youth can understand how to love his or herself and love his or her neighbor.

RESOURCE
Who is God? Loveland, Colorado, Group Publishing, 1991.

Key 12—Teaching Sticky Subjects

Youth often hide behind many sticky subjects. Youth should be taught how to cope with certain subjects. Youth often model adults. If adults cannot deal with sticky subjects, usually youth who observe these adults cannot deal with sticky subjects. In the book **Generation Next,** George Barna informs: "The behaviors and words of teens are interpreted by adults within the prevailing cultural context" (39). Youth should not totally rely upon views of their peers. The youth ministry should help youth deal with sticky subjects. Most youth go to peers for answers because youth ministry leaders often avoid discussing sticky subjects.

RESOURCE
Veerman, Dave and Others. When Kids Ask Sticky Questions— First Aid for Youth Groups, Wheaton: David C. Cook Publishing Company, 1991.

Sticky Subjects

1. Marriage	7. Male and Female
2. Divorce	8. Sexuality
3. Death and Dying	9. Drugs and Alcohol
4. Various Cultures	10. Peer Pressure
5. African History	11. Parenting
6. African Roots in Scripture	12. Planning for Life

Marriage

Discussions about marriage are often neglected because youth often select their mate. When someone selects his or her own mate, the marriage may be headed for disaster. Youth should be taught to seek God for guidance in choosing a mate. In addition to choosing a mate, youth need to understand the responsibilities of marriage. Marriage requires that both the man and woman spiritually see and know the "right" way to rear children.

RECOMMENDED RESOURCE
Wimberly, Edward P. Counseling African-American Marriages and
    Families. Louisville: Westminster John Knox Press, 1997.

Divorce

Divorce is another sticky subject. Many youth cannot deal with their parents' divorce or maybe their own divorce. The youth ministry program should teach people how to deal with their past and present problems. Even so, the program should teach that Jesus cares about all of His children.

Divorce is another topic which concerns youth. This word can be devastating to youth because many have experienced homes where divorce is a reality. Many youth come from broken homes. They need to understand that people make wrong decisions. Sometimes these wrong decisions lead to troubled marriages. In spite of decisions made, God exists to show us compassion.

Youth ministry should have sessions to teach youth how to sit down and talk to parents about divorce. A guest speaker, one who is employed as a divorce counselor, will serve well in this area. The parents must be taught to sit down and talk to children about this issue. In other words, parents should not teach children negativity such as one parent is the blame for the divorce.

RECOMMENDED RESOURCES
Nichols, J. Randall. Ending Marriage, Keeping Faith—A New Guide
    Through the Spiritual Journey of Divorce. New York: The Cross-
    road Publishing Company, 1995.

Munroe, Myles. Single, Married, Separated and Life After Divorce. Shippensburg, Pa.: Destiny Image Publishers, 1992.

Death And Dying

Death and dying are often overlooked subjects in youth ministry. The youth program should teach youth not only about life but also about death and dying. I am not sure if we are preparing for Heaven because we often hear the church discuss only life on this side. Eternal life and death and dying are rarely discussed. Youth don't have a clear conception of death and dying. Some believe death happens only to others. When death comes into one's home, youth leaders should be available to help comfort youth.

The youth ministry program should discuss the cause of death from a Christian perspective. That means teaching the Creation Story, and the story of Adam and Eve and sin, citing examples of biblical stories that involve various examples of death. Causes for death as it relates to sin should be discussed.

RECOMMENDED RESOURCES
Grollman, Earl A. Living When a Loved One has Died. Boston: Beacon Press, 1995.
Ross, Elizabeth. On Death and Dying. New York: Touchstone, 1997.
Sloyan, Virginia, editor. Death—A Source Book About Christian Death. Chicago: Liturgy Training Publications, 1990.

Various Cultures

The question of different cultures should be discussed. The African American youth should not believe that the African American is the only culture. The African American student should be taught how other cultures exist. It might be cultural shock to enter Heaven and discover that many cultures will be represented. There will not be a white or black Heaven. If we cannot begin to live and understand one another on earth, how can we live together in Heaven?

RECOMMENDED RESOURCE
Tirabassi, Maren, C. Gifts of Many Cultures—Worship Resources for the Global Community. Cleveland, United Church Press, 1995.

African History

The African history is needed for discussion. African history has, for too long, been neglected in the African American community. There is a difference between teaching the African history and non-African history. Some values are the same but some differ because we live in America. After teaching a great number of students from Africa, many African Americans do not fully understand African history. The lifestyle is quite different. If we were to live in Africa, we might not survive for a long period of time. African studies should be a part of the African American church curriculum, but not the totality of the curriculum.

RECOMMENDED RESOURCES
Paris, Peter. The Spirituality of African Peoples. Minneapolis: Augsburg Fortress, 1995.
Sertima, Ivan. Egypt—Child of Africa. New Brunswick: Transaction Publishers, 1994.

African Roots In Scripture

Of equal concern is teaching African roots in Scripture. Thanks to modern-day writers who have provided new insights about African roots in Scripture. The African American youth should be taught to understand the African roots in Scripture. Afrocentricity in Scriptures should be taught. For example, an Ethiopian eunuch brought Christianity to Africa in the first century A.D. after being baptized by Philip Acts 8:26-39.

RECOMMENDED RESOURCES
Felder, Cain Hope. Stony The Road We Trod—African-American Biblical Interpretation. Minneapolis: Fortress Press, 1991.
Ofori-Atta and M. Dixon. African Roots. Lithonia, Georgia: Third World Publishing House, 1994.

Male and Female

In addition, the African American youth should be taught how to live as a male or female. Sessions should be taught where the males and females are grouped and separate from each other. Both groups need to hear current statistics on drugs, crime, teen pregnancy, and AIDS, to list a few. According to the Kiplinger Letters, July 12, 1996 there are 14.8 Million 7-to-14-year olds and 24.9 million 18-to-24 year olds in America. **The Black Report,** a statistical book, provides the following about black males:

> At the extreme, black male youth continue to kill one another at an alarming rate. Equally distressing is the recent sharp increase in the rate of suicide among young black males. These circumstances alone have grave implications for the future of the black community. (69)

This report should encourage every youth leader to discuss with both males and females, drive by killings, gun shots, as well as other pertinent issues facing African American youth.

The following statistics are of concern among black youth:

* Unemployment among black teenagers is 2.3 times the rate for white teens. The racial unemployment gap among female teens is somewhat wider at 2.4 to 1.

* Black teenagers 15-19 years of age have a rate of 118.9 per 1000, compared to a 43.4 per 1000 rate for their white counterparts.

* Forty-two percent of black children live in poverty, 26 percent more than white children (16 percent).

* Young blacks (i.e., 24 years of age and below) are much more likely to die from homicide/legal intervention than their white counterparts.

* Black juveniles account for a greatly disproportionate number of all juvenile homicide offenders. Their representation has grown drastically during the past decade, having stood at 45 % in 1984 as to 62% in 1994.

* Blacks are also over represented among juvenile homicide victims, making up 52 percent of the total in 1994. Likewise, black juvenile homicide victims are killed predominately by firearms. Seventy-one percent died from this cause

in 1994, up from 41 percent in 1984. The corresponding figures for white victims are 56 and 38 percent.

* Blacks account for 29 percent of all juvenile arrests and an astounding 50 percent of arrests for violent crimes.
* About four-in-ten black teenagers (16-19) neither attend school nor work versus less than two-in-ten white teens.

These statistics should encourage church youth leaders to develop youth ministry teaching content around some of the current issues facing our youth.

RECOMMENDED RESOURCES

Billson, Janet M. Pathways to Manhood: Young Black Males Struggle for Identity. New York: Transaction Publishers, 1996.

Canada, Geoffrey. Reaching up for Manhood—Transforming the Lives of Boys in America. Boston: Beacon Press, 1998.

Cole, Edwin Louis. Strong Men in Tough Times—Developing Strong Character in an Age of Compromise. Lake Mary, Florida: Creation House, 1995.

Davis, Patricia H. Counseling Adolescent Girls. Minneapolis: Augsburg Fortress Press, 1996.

Hare, Bruce, Black Girls: A Comparative Analysis of Self Perception and Achievement by Race, Sex, and Socioeconomic Background. Baltimore: John Hopkins University—Center for Social Change, 1979.

Jakes, T. D. Daddy Loves His Girls. Lake Mary, Florida, Creation House, 1996 (also ask about boys, men and women books/tapes).

—So You call Yourself A Man. Tulsa: Albury Publishing, 1997.

Kunjufu, Jawanza. Countering the Conspiracy to Destroy Black Boys. Chicago: African American Images, 1985.

Madhubuti, Haki, R. Black men: Obsolete, Single, Dangerous? The African-American Family in Transition. Chicago: Third World Press—Brace Jovanich College Publishers, 1996.

Sexuality

Sexuality is another subject that the church should teach. There are many resources on this subject. It would be helpful to include discussions about sexuality. This subject should be taught because of cultural implications and because the problem exists in the world.

In a world where sex seems to be a priority, youth leaders should teach sex education, including sexually transmitted diseases. Above all, the leader should teach what the Word of God says about sex. Sex in its proper use is scriptural. Classes on sexual sins will help youth understand the scriptural purpose of sex.

RECOMMENDED RESOURCE
Boys and Girls Club of America—Act Smart Lessons, 1230 W. Peachtree Street, N.W., Atlanta, Georgia 30309; 404-815-5700.

Drugs And Alcohol

Youth need to understand the effects of drugs and alcohol. They need to hear what the Word of God states about consuming drugs and alcohol. The youth leader has a responsibility to teach youth how to escape trouble. Usually drugs and alcohol lead youth to sexual activities, which can lead to unwanted pregnancies. The youth leader should have sessions on drugs and alcohol. Bring in a speaker to speak to both parents and youth.

RECOMMENDED RESOURCE
Drugs and Drinking. Loveland: Colorado, Group Publishing, 1991.

Peer Pressure

Peer pressure is always a concern for youth. Most youth want to be a part of the crowd. Some youth will tell other youth that there is no alternative but to do what the crowd does. However, youth need to learn alternative ways to handle situations. Youth should also be taught that peer pressure is both positive and negative. In **Straight Talk On Tough Topics,** Chris Jackson writes, "Positive peer pressure also influences others to do things they would not ordinarily do. The difference between negative and positive peer pressure lies in the result of the pressure. If the pressure leads to helping the person to become worse, it's negative. If the peer pressure leads to helping the person to become better, it is positive peer pressure" (17).

Youth ministry leaders should teach youth how to distinguish positive peer pressure from negative peer pressure.

Peer pressure is often experienced intensely among youth. Many youth do not understand that peers should not affect their decisions. The youth program should teach youth to make individual decisions and to sort the good from the bad decisions that peers make. The youth program should teach youth when and when not to hang with the crowd. Just because everybody else is doing something does not make it right for the Christian youth. Every fad should not be accepted by the youth.

Youth music should be carefully selected. Some music and lyrics are not Christian in taste and often aim at mind control. When youth hear non-Christian music, they should be able to interpret the meaning of the words and understand the positive points and be able to distinguish the message from the "beat." Some youth are indiscriminate in their music choices and can be adversely affected by the lyrics in offensive songs, while others can separate the good lyrics from the bad. We have to teach youth that no music is like Christian music. At the same time, we have to teach youth that they live in a world where all kinds of music is heard. We have the wrong view that youth must tune off music altogether. In every song, something is positive, if we look for it. We should teach youth that Christian music outweighs secular music.

The church should teach youth to grow in Christ. Teens are interested in spiritual concerns. In **Generation Next,** George Barna states, "Teenagers are not flocking to Christian churches, but they are intensely interested in spiritual matters" (20). The more youth are exposed to Christian activities at home and at church, the more youth will likely recall Christian activities. The more a youth hears gospel music, the more likely will one be open to enjoy it.

RECOMMENDED RESOURCES
Jackson, Chris. <u>Straight Talk on Tough Topics.</u>

How to Handle Peer Pressure. Loveland: Colorado, Group Publishing, 1991.

Jolley, Willie. Dare to Dream—Dare to Win. Cassette. 1999. Willie Jolley Productions: PO Box 55459 DC 20040.

Parenting

Parents must be seen as parents and thus authority figures. Many youth want to be in charge of their own decisions. Many times, youth do not understand how to make needed decisions because they have not 'crossed the bridge' into adulthood. Youth should understand that it takes years to learn decision-making skills, and at one's best, one often makes poor decisions.

RECOMMENDED RESOURCES

Kesler, Jay, editor A Guide to Solving Problems and Building Relationships. Parents and Teenagers. Wheaton: Victor Books, 1984.

Morgan, Patricia. How to Raise Children of Destiny. Shippensburg, PA: Destiny Image Publishers, Inc., 1994.

Planning For Life

Planning for life is not easy. The youth leader should be concerned about the whole youth. Subjects may include:

* How to get an apartment
* How to cook
* How to set goals
* How to clean house
* How to get and keep a job
* How to relocate
* How to select and change career
* Financial management
* How to interview

RECOMMENDED RESOURCES

Edelman, Marian. The Measure of our Success—A Letter to my Children and Yours. Boston: Beacon Press, 1992.

Monroe, Myles. Seasons of Change—Understanding Purpose in Times of Perplexity. Lanham: Maryland, Pneuma Life Publishing, 1998.

Question Three: What should African American youth already involved in a youth ministry do to help other African American youth not connected to a youth ministry or church?

The established youth department in a church should teach students how to witness to others. Youth ministry should also teach students how to inform other youth about their youth ministry. Discussing exciting youth ministry events may cause other youth to attend your various activities.

Seven Ways To Deal With Realities

The following seven ways are sugggested to teach youth how to deal with realities.

1. Facing Realities
2. Envision the true picture of the Christian church
3. Attend a church and youth ministry because it is a good place to be
4. Take a second view of the pastor
5. Teach others how the Word of God supersedes personal gains
6. Learn ways to have fun in the church
7. Understand that attending youth ministry is not for self but to help others

Deciding on content for a youth ministry program is not easy. Once you have all possible resources at hand, continue to pray for the guidance of the Spirit to help determine which ones to use. There is still hope for our youth. Reading a book by Dave Burrows entitled, **Talk To Me**, reminds me of the realities for youth that we often overlook. Leaders who plan content for youth lessons must rethink content planning. Many times the church faces a mask hiding the problems that beset our youth. It is true that others are trying to capture them or distract them from their Christian walk. For example, if youth don't experience non-Christian life in the real world, they will experience it on television. The youth ministry program must teach youth how to avoid the battles at hand. Every city, every town, and every rural, urban or suburban area has its similar problems for youth. Why wait until the problems are at hand with your youth before you consider waking up and plan a program for them? Save as many youth as you can by preparing in advance.

Facing Realities

Youth leaders should remember that they provide experiences for youth. It is likely that youth leaders have been, at some point, exposed to the realities that youth experience. The realities are created in this world before today's youth were born. Youth leaders should help youth deal with these realities. For example, discuss the real events impacting and impressing upon youth like turning the death of a rap star into a discussion about the positive and negative aspects of Rap music. The positive side is that God loves and cares for all. The negative side might promote or reinforce violence.

Points to Remember

By permission
1. Teenagers don't go to Columbia and fly drugs across the Atlantic for sale and distribution.
2. Teenagers don't write television shows or movies.
3. Teenagers are indelibly influenced by what is written and done by adults.
4. If parents want to know what is wrong with their children, they should look in the mirror of their lives and multiply what they see.
5. The world today is reaping a bitter harvest. This harvest is born of parents in an irresponsible society and reaped in teenagers who are out of order.
6. There are still Daniels, Shadrachs, Meschachs and Abednegos, Timothys, Davids and countless others who know the truth, who will go with God and who will make the difference (Burrows 10).

Other Realities
Points to Remember

By permission
1. Teens want to have fun.
2. God likes what you like.
3. God does not have a type of music that He has placed upon His Body and said, 'Play this only.'
   Christian music is more what you say than how you play.
4. God is too big to fit into a single culture, style or fashion.
5. Ensure that the music you listen to is good seed for your mind and spirit.
6. Watch the lifestyles of and read up on Christian and other artists. Don't listen to or support musicians, Christian or not, who don't seem to care about how they live.
7. We need to learn to praise as much as we learn to jam. We need to learn to worship before we celebrate.
8. Our music needs to help us communicate with God and should further our relationships with Him.
9. Television is not evil; it is what's on the TV and who is controlling it that's evil.
10. Christians should own more stations; then we can say more about what should be on television.
11. The movies and television programs you watch need to be compared to the values of the Bible. If the values espoused by a movie or television program are contrary to God's Word, you as a citizen of a higher kingdom should not watch or support it.
12. Dance can be fun, creative and as unto the Lord. But like so many other things, it gets lost in a maze of abuse of its original purpose.
13. We should never substitute entertainment for substance. (Burrows 72-73)

Envision the True Picture of the Christian Church

The youth program should teach youth what the church is really about. There have been many false perceptions about the church. Rarely does one hear about the positive things that go on in the church. The youth program must assure youth that the African American church is still the most noted institution in the African American community. Youth ministry should teach youth what the church is all about, correct the distorted views, i.e., everybody behaves nicely and treats others nicely. The church is the spiritual headquarters for life. It is the hospital where spiritually sick people are recovering. We all have faults but we are in the hospital to get well. Some are in the emergency room, some are in intensive care, some are walking around doing well, some appear to have no pain but are inwardly hurting and some are ready to go home but are still awaiting the death angel. Whatever the case may be, we are all hospitalized, seeking some type of help. The African American church should train the youth ministry team to care for the spiritually sick. In training and working, many workers may become sick, but the life of the church goes on.

Attend Church and Youth Ministry Because it is a Good Place to Be

Youth involved in youth programs should tell other youth that the church is really a good place to be, because it is where the Word of God and spiritual nourishment are provided. It is also a place of peace and calmness. In many settings, which all should be, youth can retire from destructive or chaotic environment and rethink life. The church should allow youth to think about the future and eternal rest. Youth ministry is a place to learn and comprehend that everybody has something positive and negative in their lives. Dr. Sandra Taylor-Griffin wrote a doctoral thesis on "Refuges from Racism: Adolescent Community Settings As An Early Motivational Influence for High Achieving Black Men." She states, "Historically, black churches have provided sanctuary and positive direction for their members" (170-171). Still, youth ministry is a place to cry, shout, have fun together and learn from each other.

RESOURCE
Costen, Melva Wilson. <u>African-American Christian Worship</u>. Nashville: Abingdon Press, 1993.

Take A Second View of the Pastor

The youth leader has a major responsibility to teach youth the role of the pastor. A youth connected with a youth minister can help other youth take a second look at the pastor by sharing positive points about the pastor. The youth must be taught to avoid agreeing with negative statements about the pastor. The pastor does not serve part, but the entire congregation. The pastor is responsible for wearing a lot of hats. He or she might have associates or assistants, but no worker's responsibility replaces the work of a pastor.

A youth member might inform other youth not only about the role of the minister but also teach others that the church is responsible for taking care of the pastor's needs. The pastor's vocation is his profession and whereas the ministry takes priority, other concerns should not circumvent him from engaging in effective ministry.

Teach Others How The Word Of God Supersedes Personal Gains

It would be so wonderful to have youth to teach other youth about personal gains. Some youth think that living is all about personal gains. But life is not about the automobile, the houses, sweaters, sports jackets or jewelry, all of which are good when put in the right priority, but our first debt is to God. God owns everything. Youth involved in a youth ministry can tell others how the Word of God supersedes everything else. Seeking first the kingdom of God allows one to respect the Word of God. Allowing the Word of God to supersede personal gains will cause one to attend church services and youth activities of the church. This hunger, when properly taught, will teach youth that church is more than attending a service one day a week. If one attends regular church services, he or she has not done enough for God. Every Christian should consider participating in other church activities in order to have a holistic experience. These activities are beyond our duty to Bible and Prayer Services. The more one is exposed to the Word of God, the more one will seek God's guidance; yet youth need to be reminded that even at their best, Satan will attempt to distract them.

Learn Ways to Have Fun in the Church

Youth can help other youth to know that church can be fun. It is not a place to come and look pretty. Church should be a place where the whole person, whole body, can benefit. In other words, the church is a place where fitness and health programs should exist, where new information can be shared, where youth can understand that all rap music is not bad and where they can be introduced to Christian artists. Theater and dance ministries are needed in today's church. The church must allow youth and others to present their talents in a Christian fashion.

The African American church should open its doors for gospel recording artists and for new talent. Writers should be presented for book-signing as a way to introduce Christian writers to the church. Many authors have a good message. If we are going to encourage church members to buy and use books at other times, why not become familiar with the authors? Many leaders use manuals such as The Hiscox Guide. Do you know the author? Do you know who wrote the Articles of Faith? Often choir members don't know the authors or the meanings of the songs they sing. The African

American church is still the place to introduce black culture by exploring the answers to these questions.

Understand that Attending Youth Ministry Is Not For Yourself But to Help Others

Every youth member should understand why he or she attends the church and youth ministry. One attends youth ministry not to help self but to benefit others. Do not attend class just to learn, but to tell others about what you have learned as well. Our existence is then not for self-glory but to glorify God and to help others to learn that we are servants, not for self, but for others.

CHAPTER FIVE

Twenty-One Youth Discussion Topics

There are numerous topics to be discussed with youth. The youth ministry program should provide discussions on various topics. Many of these topics are already discussed. This list is only a starting point for a youth ministry. You may add or delete topics to meet the needs of your youth ministry. It is very important to provide discussions that are around current needs. All discussions should be handled with much care. A training workshop for leaders might be held to teach leaders how to lead group discussions. Twenty-one topics are:

1. Television/movies
2. Rap music
3. Gospel music
4. Alcohol and drugs
5. Culture
6. African history
7. History of blacks in America
8. Dealing with personal problems
9. What to keep to yourself
10. Patience
11. Obeying parental rules
12. When to say no to friends
13. Responsibilities of living on your own
14. Grief
15. Budgeting
16. Choosing friends
17. Choosing activities
18. How to help mom
19. How to help dad
20. Learning how to fast
21. Learning how to read the Bible

CHAPTER SIX

Twelve Youth Discussion Topics For Parents/Guardians

Parents or guardians should be familiar youth concerns and needs. At some point the youth ministry program should teach parents how to sit down at the table with youth. Parents and youth must work as a team rather than against each other. The youth ministry program should teach parents and youth how to work as a team rather than as separate persons. Each must have respect for one another. The youth should be taught that the parent or guardian is the head of the household and that God requires obedience. We all have to abide by rules we do not like. Youth must also abide by many rules they disagree with. Rather than fighting and fussing, the youth program should teach family values and ways for the family to work as a unit. Some topics for parents or guardians include:

1. What can I/we do to help youth?
2. How can I show more love toward youth?
3. What are my alternatives if plan one fails?
4. What rules should I have and how should I discuss them with youth?
5. Thinking before acting
6. The Bible as your spiritual road map
7. Providing a new change for today's youth
8. Learning to let go of the past
9. Youth of today can make it, in spite of obstacles
10. How to live a godly life
11. How do I confront youth when they get in trouble or violate rules?
12. How many times are enough?

Play Ball

By permission:
Mr. Aron Liles, youth leader, Atlanta, Georgia

Being a young man you learned basketball,
   on streets of a city you learned least of all;
As you tie your Jordan's, FILA's or Nike's to play,
   get on your knees before each game to pray;
You play that starter jacket and starter cap,
   please help us Jesus learn this religious rap...
   Uh Huh, Uh Huh
   Jesus Christ makes you wanna Jump Jump!
   His Father makes you wanna Jump Jump!
   Holy Spirit makes you wanna Jump Jump!
   This prayer makes you wanna Jump Jump!
Can't be no man by the things you do,
   believe in Jesus, He's gonna help you;
Don't need no gun, just to have some fun,
   junk called crack, keeps you on the run.
All them streets are full of dope,
   we all need Jesus, faith and hope...
   Uh Huh, Uh Huh
   Jesus Christ makes you wanna Jump Jump!
   His Father makes you wanna Jump Jump!
   Holy Spirit makes you wanna Jump Jump!
   This prayer makes you wanna Jump Jump!
With Jesus as coach we play to win,
   this game on His court, He'll let us in;
A new game starts each and every day,
   thank God for that, in Jesus' name we pray...
   Jesus Christ makes you wanna Jump Jump!
   Thank God you wanna Jump Jump!
   Dear Lord, let us Jump Jump!
   Thanks to Jesus we can Jump Jump!...
   Uh Huh, Uh Huh!
Play ...Ball...Jump...Jump!!!

Appendix

These forms are only suggestions for the youth team. Some may be modified to meet the needs of a given youth ministry. I am not responsible for any form that is used by any youth ministry team. These forms are only guides to help leaders develop their own forms.

Sample Forms For Youth Work

1. Sample goals
2. Sample objectives
3. Agenda concerns
4. Preparing the youth ministry meeting
5. Sample of the opening announcement
6. Meeting the youth
7. Meeting the parent
8. Learning more about youth
9. More questions to learn
10. How much do you know about your faith?
11. Thinking through the questions on faith
12. Sample volunteer staff
13. Sample medical and liability release
14. Sample of legality requirement
15. Volunteer Paid staff application
16. Sample congregational and community youth ministry survey
17. Community youth ministry history
18. Sample permission to travel
19. Sample long and overnight trip application
20. Sample permission to participate in youth activities
21. Sample youth agreement

Form One

Goals

1. **Example One:** Youth will appreciate studying/reading the Bible.
2. **Example Two:** Youth will learn to appreciate the difference between worldly and Christian behavior.
3. **Example Three:** Youth will learn how to develop a meaningful prayer life.

Form Two

Objectives

Looking at your goal, what are three objectives for your youth?

Example One:

a. Youth will be taught ways to study the Bible by attending five class sessions on "How to Study the Bible."
b. Youth will be able to list all books of the Old Testament in chronological order.
c. Youth will participate in activities that will enhance their thinking on how to study the Bible.

Example Two:

a. Youth will attend six sessions to hear lectures and participate in discussion on "Youth in the World" vs. "Youth in the church."
b. Following an introduction, youth will write four Scripture references that relate to Christian behavior.

Example Three:

a. Youth will read two books (in three months) on the power of prayer.
b. Youth will write two definitions for the term Prayer.

More information on goals and objectives may be read in the book, **Teacher Training in the African-American Church,** by Dr. Oneal Sandidge.

Form Three

Agenda Concerns

Items on the agenda below will be covered over several meetings.

1. Opening song or poem or story
2. Scripture
3. Prayer
4. Minutes from the last session

   The above four things should take place at every youth meeting.
5. Discuss budget:
   a. How monies will be distributed
   b. How monies will be requested for youth ministry
   c. Funds included in the budget for conferences, retreats, and other events
   d. The church's policy about fund raising, tickets for bus trips, and other activities. The leader should have an understanding about budgetary guidelines.
6. Discuss the agenda for the opening night.
7. Discuss the announcement for the first youth meeting.
8. Closing prayer

Form Four

Planning Committee—For Youth Opening Night

1. Opening song or poem or story
2. Scripture
3. Prayer
4. Nominations for the planning committee (This committee will review the first meeting and suggest an agenda to the youth minister for the next meeting. The youth minister will plan subsequent meetings.)
5 Nominate a secretary to take minutes.
6. Objectives for the youth ministry
7. Discuss all details for the opening event.
8. Closing prayer

Form Five

The Opening Announcement

JOIN US FOR FUN
GAMES
AND NEW RELATIONSHIPS

When:

Where:

Time:

Come early for a good seat!

For more information call:

Form Six

Meeting the youth

Please print!

Name _____ Age _____

Male/Female _____

Address _____

City/State/Zip _____

Phone _____ Date of Birth _____

1. What school do you attend during the week? _____
2. What is your favorite subject?_____
3. How many brothers and sisters do you have?
4. Brothers   _____ _____ _____ _____
5. Sisters   _____ _____ _____ _____
6. Do you know your father's and mother's first and last names? Yes.___ No.___ If yes, what?_____
7. Do you know with whom you live? Yes.___ No.___
8. With whom do you live? _____
9. How many years have you lived in this area? _____
10. How did you hear about this youth program?_____
11. What one thing are you seeking from this program?__
12. Are you a leader or follower?_____
13. Do know anyone who attends this youth program? Who? _____
14. What do you like about church? _____
15. Is there anything you dislike about church?_____
16. If you were to change one thing in the church, what would it be?
17. What is your favorite hobby? _____
18. What is your favorite sport? _____
19. In sports, who is your favorite team? _____

Form Seven-A

Meeting The Parent
Chart For The Mother or Female Guardian

1. Name of mother or guardian:

2. The address of mother or guardian:

3. Telephone number of mother or guardian:

4. Hobbies of mother or guardian:

5. The name of church where mother or guardian has membership:

6. Length of time mother or guardian has lived with youth:

7. How much time do you spend with your youth per week?

8. Do you attend any activities with your youth? What activities? How often?

9. Do you eat meals at the same table? At the same time?

10. Do you watch television with your youth?

Form Seven-B

Meeting The Parent
For The Father or Male Guardian

1. The name of father or guardian:

2. The address of father or guardian:

3. Telephone number of father or guardian:

4. Hobbies of father or guardian:

5. The church where father or guardian has membership:

6. How long a member:

7. Length of time father or guardian has lived with youth:

8. How much time do you spend with your youth per week?:

9. Do you attend any activities with your youth? What activities? How often?

10. Do you eat meals at the same table? At the same time?

11. Do you watch television with your youth?

Form Eight

Learning More About You

Name _____

Name preferred to be called _____

___Male ___Female ___Age ___Height ___Weight

Street Address _____

City/State/ Zip _____

Phone_____ Date of Birth _____

1. Do you ever fight your friends/relatives?_____
2. What is your favorite TV program?_____
3. Do you have a hobby? If so, what is it?_____
4. What is your special cologne? _____
5. Are you attending a church? ___Yes ___No
6. How long have you been affiliated with the church?__
7. Is your guardian a member, or are your parents members of a church? ___Yes ___No
8. Are there any members in your family, ages 12 or more, who are not part of this church? ___Yes ___No
9. What time are you required to be home on weekends?____
10. Do you like Pizza? ___Yes ___No
11. Are you a member of any gang?___Yes ___No
12. Have you been a member of a gang? ___Yes ___No
13. Have you ever gotten drunk just for the fun of it? ___Yes ___No
14. Have you ever experienced drugs?___Yes ___No
15. What is your favorite kind of music? _____
16. Do you read the Bible? ___Often?
    ___Sometimes? ___Seldom ___Never

Form Nine

More To Learn

1. Have you been baptized? ___Yes ___No

2. Have you ever attended a new member's class?
   ___Yes ___No

3. Check all that you believe: Would you say that God is:
   ___alive ___dead ___something that exists
   ___all powerful. ___the Father of us all
   ___the Mother of us all ___the Father/Mother of us all

4. Is Jesus the Son of God? ___Yes ___No

5. Do you believe that hell exists? ___Yes ___No
   ___Maybe

6. Do you believe that heaven exists? ___Yes ___No

7. Have you ever read more than two entire books of
   the Bible? ___Yes ___No

8. Can one die and go to heaven without knowing God?
   ___Yes ___No

9. Should Christian attempt to share their faith with
   other people? ___Yes ___No

10. Do you know a Bible verse? ___Yes ___No

11. What do you think about other religions, i.e., Muslims? _____

12. What one thing do you not understand about serving God?

13. What is the Holy Spirit? _____

14. Are you saved? ___Yes ___No

Form Ten

How much do you know about your faith?

Quoted by permission from: Beundschuh, Rick and Trutzschler, E. G., **Incredible! Questionnaires For Youth.** Grand Rapids, Michigan, Zondervan Publishing House, 1995.

1. You must be baptized in order to be a Christian.
   ___Yes ___ No
2. The best definition of grace is: (check one)
   ___A prayer said at mealtime
   ___Something kind, gentle, and sweet
   ___Getting something you don't deserve
   ___God's sympathy or compassion
3. You cannot be sure that you are really saved until Judgment Day. Can___ Can't___
4. The word "trinity" is found in the Bible. ___Yes___No
5. Jesus was in existence before He was born in Bethlehem. ___Yes ___No
6. The best definition of repentance is: (check one) ___Being sorry for what you did wrong ___Turning and going the other way ___Making up for all the wrong you have done ___Telling God you are sorry in an overt, emotional way
7. Blasphemy of the Holy Spirit is the only sin that cannot be forgiven. ___Yes ___No
8. The Bible forbids Christians to drink alcoholic beverages. ___Yes ___No
9. A person can be a follower of both Christ and Buddha. ___Yes ___ No
10. A minister or missionary is closer to God than "ordinary" Christians. ___Yes ___No
11. No one has ever seen God the Father. ___Some have ___No one has
12. Jesus was 100 percent man and 100 percent God. ___Yes ___ No

13. All people are born with the stain of sin upon them.
    ___Yes ___ No
14. People become angels when they die. ___Yes ___No
15. Jesus was taken to Egypt as a small child. ___Yes ___No
16. Three wise men visited Christ shortly after His birth.
    ___Yes ___No
17. Jesus was known to get angry. ___Yes ___No
18. After His death and resurrection, how long did Jesus
    appear to people before He ascended to heaven?
    ___3 days ___20 days ___40 days ___50 days

Form Eleven

Thinking through the Questions on Faith Answers:

1. No. The thief on the cross was not baptized (see Luke 23:39-43)
2. Getting something you don't deserve (see Ephesians 1:7-8)
3. Can (see 1 John 5:11-12)
4. No
5. Yes (see John 8:56-58)
6. Turning and going the other way
7. Yes (see Matthew 12:31)
8. No (see 1 Timothy 5:23)
9. No (see John 14:6; Acts 4:12)
10. No, not necessarily. For example, the thief on the cross (see Luke 23:39-43) and the apostle Paul (see Acts 9:1-2)
11. No one has (see 1 Timothy 6:15-16)
12. Yes (see John 1:1,14; Philippians 2:5-7; Hebrews 2:14)
13. Yes (see Romans 5:12, 19)
14. No, Scripture never indicates this
15. Yes (see Matthew 2:13-15)
16. No, the number is never given
17. Yes (see John 2:14-16)
18. Forty days (see Acts 1:3)

Form Twelve

Sample Volunteer Staff Contract

I agree to serve as a youth worker school staff for six months (Some leaders may need to test their abilities before signing a contract for an extended time) beginning on _____. I agree to abide by the following:

a. To attend regular worship services.
b. To attend all staff meetings.
c. To be on time for youth leadership responsibilities.
d. To attend at least half of the social functions.
e. To attend at least one field trip function.
f. To be in contact with all parents at least every three months.
g. To contact any youth who misses two meetings.
h. To abide by the leadership of this group.
i. To adhere to and respect the pastor of this church.
j. To inform the leader and substitute, when possible, three days in advance about being absent.
k. To give a one-month notice, should I decide to resign this position?
l. To turn in lesson plans on time.
m. If a leader is not capable of the job, he or she will be given a 60-days trail period. Either party may request the resignation without any commitment.
n. To complete and turn in any required paperwork—letters/responses—immediately within one week of receipt.
o. To seek training to constantly up-date my skills for working with youth.

Signed:
Worker Leader
Copies for the file and for the worker

Form Thirteen

Sample medical and liability release

(Should be printed on the church's letterhead)

   It is also recommended to seek medical forms from physicians in your state. Medical laws may change from state to state.

Name _____Age ____

Address_____

City/State_____Zip _____Phone_____

In emergency, notify _____

Phone _____

Doctor _____ City_____

Phone _____

Health history:

* Allergies: List any _____

* Other conditions: ___Heart ___Frequent colds

* Chronic conditions: ___Asthma
      ___Frequent Diabetes, ___Epilepsy, ___stomach

* Physical problems: ___High Blood Pressure

* Other _____

If you checked any of the above, please give details (i.e., include normal treatment of allergic reactions):

* Date of last tetanus shot: /   /

* Name and dosage of any medications that must be
  taken:_____

* Any swimming restrictions: ___Yes ___No

* Any activity restrictions: ___Yes ___No

* What restrictions?

* Anything else that we should know?

Name and address of your primary care doctor? _____

Address of your doctor? _____

Telephone number of your doctor?_____

Form Fourteen

Note: Consult legal advice for forms appropriate for your state.

Our church will not be responsible for any medical payment, unless accident occurs on behalf of the church. If you have medical insurance, your carrier will be billed for medical charges in the case of illness or injury while your son or daughter is on a church-related activity. If you do not have medical insurance, you will be billed by the medical facility.

In addition to the above, the church usually has an attorney to consult. The youth leader should have some professional agreement available for the church. In addition, those who work with children should be tested for drugs and have completed criminal/background checks. If committed a crime, Christ forgives. The leader/pastor must carefully allow the Spirit to guide in making such a crucial decision.

_____ Name of child

_____ Name of parent

Form Fifteen

Volunteer/Paid Staff Application

Check One: ___Volunteer ___Paid Staff Position

Name _____

Address_____City____Zip _____Phone_____

Occupation _____

Marital status _____Birth date _____

How long have you been at this church? _____

1. Give a brief account as to how you became a Christian:

2. Why do you feel led to work with young people?

3. If you could do anything in youth ministry, what would you like to do? List your top three desires:
   a.
   b.
   c.
4. What kind of ministry experience do you have?
5. What is your educational background?
6. What are your three favorite hobbies/interests?
   a.
   b.
   c.
7. What situations have you had to work through in your personal life that you can use in ministering to young people?
8. Describe your devotional life:
9. Describe your family life:
10. In what ways would you like the Church/Pastor to minister to you during the time you serve the youth?

Form Sixteen

A Congregational and Community Youth Ministry Survey

Purpose: Identify the past and present state of youth ministry in a congregation and community.

Congregational youth ministry history

Focus on the last five to ten years. Speak with six to nine key people:

A. A former pastor.
B. Two high school students active in the church.
C. Two young adults who grew up in the church.
D. Two parents of young adults.
E. A past president of the congregation.
F. A youth and young adult leader from the past.
G. Two confirmands.
H. Follow the suggestions of these people as to who might know more.

These questions might be asked:

1. Where have youth been present in the life of the congregation?
2. What has been the congregation's attitude about youth?
3. How have young people and their parents viewed the confirmation ministry?
4. Have young people respected and valued the pastor?
5. Have young people felt welcome here?
6. Has there been a youth program? A youth group? Name these persons who were involved?
7. Who's been involved? What's it been like? Please provide two to three memorable moments.
8. What contribution has this congregation made in the lives of young people?
9. Who has been responsible for youth ministry?

Form Seventeen

Community Youth Ministry History

Focus on the last five to ten years. Speak to a representative person from each congregation, parachurch group, and ecumenical agency in the community. The group listed above might also be asked these questions:

1. Where have youth (particularly Christian youth) been present in the life of the community?
2. How are youth perceived in the community?
3. What is your congregation, group, or agency doing in ministry with youth?
4. What contributions are youth (particularly Christian youth) making in the community?
5. What needs of youth are being/not being met in the community?
6. What are the community's institutions' (school, law enforcement, business, social service, etc.) attitudes about the churches', parachurch groups', and ecumenical agencies' work with youth?

Congregational and Community Uouth Summary, Analysis, and Implications

A. Develop a summary of the findings.
B. Analysis: Look at strengths, weaknesses, assumptions, possible resources, and coalitions as well as challenges.
C. Draw implications for the future.

The findings of this survey will guide the congregation's youth ministry representative and pastor in taking the next steps in their development of the congregation's ministry with youth.

Martinson, Roland D. Effective Youth Ministry—A Congregational Approach. Minneapolis: Augsburg Publishing House, 1988, appendix 141-143. Used by permission.

Form Eighteen

Permission to Travel Form

Forms for major trips during the course of the year are needed for any church. For example, in some cases, taking a youth to the store may be risky, but not in all cases. One must allow the Holy Spirit to rule. One writer states: "Avoid overkill. Parental permission slips for a trip to the corner fast food joint is probably overkill" (Bundschuh 43).

- Permission to travel
- Name of youth group:
- Name of Youth:
- Departing from:
- Destination:
- Purpose of trip:

- Departing time:
- Returning time:
- Parental approval signature:
- Youth leader signature:
- Liability / insurance:

Form Nineteen

Long and Overnight Trip Application

Details about the trip:
1. Clothing
2. If overnight, all details: hotel information, phone numbers where you are going, food needed, money needed for food, spending money suggested and any other details. A copy of brochures and more specific information about sites, means of transportation, chaperons, and what's not allowed would be helpful.
3. Make sure to inform youth and parents about total costs, payment dates, cancellation fees, return of monies, and all other deadlines for the trip.

Form Twenty

Permission To Participate In Youth Activities Form

This youth group _____ (name) will not be responsible for any damage incurred from youth participating in youth activities. Participation is "free will."

Permission is being granted for _____(name of youth) to participate in youth activities sponsored by _____ (name of Church).
_____ Name of guardian/parent
_____Name of youth leader

Form Twenty One

Youth Agreement

This agreement is between_____(name of youth) and _____(name of youth group) represented by _____ (name of youth leader) to work together in the named youth group to enhance spiritual skills for Christian living. It is understood that either party may cancel the duration of membership.

_____
Signature of youth

_____
Signature of youth leader

_____
Signature of guardian/parent

Date: _____/_____/_____

Sources Cited

Arterburn, Stephen and Burns, Jim. **Drug Proof Your Kid.** Ventura California: Regal Books, 1995.

Barna, George. **Generation Next.** Ventura, California: Regal Books, 1995.

Bertolini, Dewey M. **Back to the Heart of Youth Work.** Wheaton, Illinois: Victor Books, 1984.

Burns, Jim. **The Youth Builder.** Eugene, Oregon: Harvest House Publishers, 1988.

Burrows, Dave. **Talk To Me.** Shippensburg, PA: Destiny Image Publishers, 1996.

Cully, Iris and Cully, Kendig editors. **Harper's Encyclopedia of Religious Education.** New York: Harper and Row, Publishers Inc., 1990.

Dunn, Rick. **"What are the Necessary Competencies To Be An Effective Youth Worker?"** Christian Education Journal, Volume XVI, Number 3, Spring 1996, p. 30.

Fields, Doug. **Help! I'm A Volunteer Youth Worker!** Grand Rapids: Zondervan Publishers, 1992.

Freeman, Darrell, Sr. **Investing in our African-American Youth—Can You Handle It?** Wilmington, Delaware: Truth Bible Institute, 1994.

Foster, Charles. **Walking with Black Youth.** Nashville: Abingdom Press, 1989.

Griend, Alvin. **Discover Your Gifts and Learn How to Use Them.** Grand Rapids: CRC Publications, 1996.

Jackson, Chris. **Straight Talk on Tough Topics.** Grand Rapids: Zondervan Publishing, 1996.

Kageler, Len. **How to Expand Your Youth Ministry—Practical Ways to Increase Your Attendance.** Grand Rapids: Zondervan, 1996.

Lamport, Mark, A. **"What is Youth Ministry"** Christian Education Journal, Volume XVI, Number 3, Spring 1996, p. 62.

Martinson, Roland, D. **Effective Youth Ministry—A Congregational Approach.** Minneapolis: Augsburg Publishing House, 1988.

McDowell, Josh and Hostetler, Bob. **Don't Check Your Brains at the Door.** Dallas: Word Publishing, 1992.

Mitchell, Henry and Emil Thomas. **Preaching for Black Self-Esteem.** Nashville: Abingdon Press, 1994.

Nichols, Charles, H. "The Learner: Youth" in **Introduction to Biblical Christian Education.** Edited by Werner Graendorf. Chicago: Moody Bible Institute, 1981.

Perkins, John M. **Restoring At Risk Communities—Doing It Together and Doing It Right.** Grand Rapids: Baker Books,1995.

Tidwell, Billy. **The Black Report.** Lanham, Maryland: Unversity Press, 1997.

Trutzchler, E. G. Von and Bundschuh. **A Youth Ministry Crash Course,** Grand Rapids, Zondervan Publishing Company, 1996.

Walker, Clarence. **Breaking Strongholds in the African-American Family—Strategies for Spiritual Warfare.** Grand Rapids, Zondervan Publishing House, 1996.

RECOMMENDED RESOURCES
FOR YOUTH MINISTRY PLANNING

Note: These are only suggested resources. I am not endorsing any work nor do I agree with every statement in the books recommended.

Black/African American Resources

At-risk Youth, At-risk Church: What Jesus Christ and American teenagers are saying to the mainline church. Princeton: Institute for Youth Ministry, Princeton Theological Seminary, 1998.

Foster, Charles and Shockley, Grant. **Working with Black Youth.** Nashville: Abingdon Press, 1990.

Johnson, Lou. **Christian Rites of a Passage for African-American Youth.** D.Min. dissertation, United Theological Seminary, 1997.

Jones, Reginald. **Black Adolescents.** Berkeley: Cobb and Henry Publishers, 1989.

Kalonji, Stephanie. **Umoja Youth Minictry:** An educational youth progam for African-American churches, MA Thesis, Catholic Theological Union at Chicago, 1999.

Kunjufu, Jawanza. **Countering the Conspiracy To destroy Black Boys.** Chicago: African-American Images, 1985.

Mason, Henry L. A couseling intervention model for ministry to African-American male juvenile offers: Ages 10-17. D.Min. dissertation, United Theological Seminary, 1998.

McCray, Walter. **Reaching and Teaching Black Young Adults.** Chicago, Black Light Fellowship, 1966.

Morgan, Patricia. **How To raise Children of Destiny.** Shippensburg, PA: Destiny Image, 1995.

Multimedia Production. **Skills for the African-American Church Media Ministry.** D.Min. dissertation, United Theological Seminary, 1997.

Munroe, Myles. **Single, Married, Separated and Life After Divorce.** Shippensburg, PA: Destiny Image, 1997.

Redmond, Dyke H. **The Empowerment of Youth —Restoring Hope.** Boston: Beacon Press, 1997.

Smith, James Garfield, III. **Reversing an environment of mistrust:** Urban Church Ministries which create positive relationships between police and African-American youth. D.Min. dissertation, United Theological Seminary, 1998.

Smith, Jessis and Robert Johns. **Statistical Record of Black Americans.**

Tehran, Frazier. **Transforming Ministry with African-American Inner City Youth.** D.Min. dissertation, Claremont School of Theology, 1998.

Turner, Ronald F. **Developing the African American Male Child.** D.Min. dissertation, United Theological Seminary, 1995.

Walker, Clarence. **Biblical Counseling with African-Americans.** Grand Rapids: Zondervan, 1992.

West, Cornel. **Race Matters.** Boston: Beacon Press, 1993.
— **Restoring Hope.** Boston: Beacon Press, 1997.
Wilson, Ames. **The Developmental Psychology of the Black Child.** New York: Africara Research Publication

Retreats

Cannon, Chris, editor. **Great Retreats for Youth Groups— 12 Complete Faith-Building Week-Ends.** Grand Rapids: Zondervan Publishing, 1994.

Ideas

1. Rice, Wayne and Yaconelli, Mike. **Holiday Ideas for Youth Groups.** Grand Rapids: Zondervan Publishing, 1981.
2. Ibid. **Incredible Ideas for Youth Groups.** Grand Rapids: Zondervan, 1981.
3. Sparks, Lee. **The Youth Group How-To Book,** Loveland, Colorado, Group Books, 1981.

General Counseling

1. Olson, Arvis. **Sexuality: Guidelines for Teenagers,** Grand Rapids, Baker, 1981.
2. Burns, Jim. **The Youth Builder,** Eugene, OR: Harvest House, 1988.
3. Olson, Keith. **Counseling Teenagers,** Loveland, Colorado., Group Books, 1984.

Other Resources For Youth Ministry

1. Group Publishing, Box 481, Loveland, CO 80539
2. Youth Specialties, 1224 Greenfield Drive, El Cajon, CA 92021
3. David C. Cook Publishing Company, Scripture Press, 4050 Lee Vance View Colorado Springs, CO 80918
4. Harvest House Publishers, LifeSources for Youth Material, 1075 Arrowsmith Eugene, OR 97402
5. National Network of Youth Ministries, Box 26146, San Diego, CA 92126

6. National Institute of Youth Ministry, 24422 Del Prado #12, Dana Point, CA 92629
7. See You AT The Party Video, Josh McDowell's Video
8. *Christian Education Journal,* Autumn 1988 Vol. IX No. 1 "Identifying Formation—Theory and Youth Ministry," Winter 1991, Vol. XI, no.2 "Understanding Today's Youth Culture"
9. *Sexuality Education: Techniques, Methodologies,* Curricula: Morrison, Eleanor and Mila Price. New York: Duxbury Press, 1974 . Write to Planned Parenthood of Santa Cruz County, 421 Ocean Street, Santa Cruz 95060 $10.00 + 1.00 Shipping
10. Myers, William, R. **Black and White Styles of Youth Ministry—Two Congregations in American.** New York: Pilgrim Press, 1991.
11. Chu, Thomas, K. and others. **God Works.** Harrisburg: Morehouse Publishing, 1997.
12. *Act Smart—HIV/AIDS Education Curriculum Resource,* Boys and Girls Club of American, National Headquarters 1230 W. Peachtree Street, Atlanta, GA 30309 404-815-5700
13. National Association of Sef-Esteem 1-800-488 NASE

Other African American Resources

1. David C. Cook Publishing Company
   Echoes Division
   4050 Lee Vance View
   Colorado Springs, CO 80918
2. Sonlight Productions
   Youth Ministry
   1613 W. Washington Blvd
   Chicago, Illinois 60612 312-733-3841
3. National Black Christian Students Conference
   P.O. Box 4311
   Chicago, Illinois 60680 312-722-0236
4. Christian Education Enrichment Center
   1439 W. 103rd Street
   Chicago, Illinois 60643

5. Renaissance Productions
   537 Mantua Ave., Suite 203
   Woodbury, New Jersey 08096 1-800-234-2338
6. Urban Ministries, Chicago, Illinois
7. Multi-Cultural Resources Center
   Scarritt Graduate School
   1008 19th Avenue, South
   Nashville, Tennessee 37203
8. Directory of African-American Religious Bodies
   Howard University School of Divinity
   Order from 2200 Girard Ave.
   Baltimore, MD 2121, Phone: 410-516-6947

Films
ROA Films
   1696 North Astor Street
   Milwaukee, WI 53202
Word Publishing
   Box 1790
   Waco, TX 76796

Hotlines
* National Drug and Alcohol Help Line, 1-800-821-4357.
* National Runaway Switchboard 1-800-621-4000
* Rainn Rape Abuse National Network, 1-800-656-HOPE.
* Covenant House 1-800-999-9999 (ask for additional aids
  for youth).
* National Domestic Violence Hotline, 1-800-799-7233.
* Families Anonymous, 1-800-736-9805.
* National AIDS Hotline, 1-800-342-2437

Resources and Organizations to prevent youth violence in
  America
* Alcohol and Drug Abuse Hotline, 1-800-237-6237
* Boys Town National Hotline, 1-800-448-3000
* Center to Prevent Handgun Violence, 1-202-898-0792
* Child Abuse Hotline, 1-800-540-4000

* Child Help USA, 1-800-422-4453
* Children Now, 1-800-CHILD-44 (244-5344)
* Coalition to Stop Gun Violence, 1-202-544-7190
* Crisis Counseling Hotline, 1-800-444-9999
* National Clearinghouse for Alcohol
  and Drug Information, 1-800-729-6686
* National Council for Child Abuse
  and Family Violence, 1-800-222-2000
* Natinal Crime Prevention Council, 1-202-466-6272
* National Institute on Drug Abuse
  Referral Hotline, 1-800-662-HELP (662-4357)
* National Victim Center INFOLINK,
  1-800-FYI-CALL (394-2255)
* NINE LINE (help line for youth) 1-800-999-9999
* Runaway Hotline, 1-800-231-6946
* Suicide Prevention Hotline, 1-800-827-7571
* Violence Prevention Coalition, 1-213-240-7785

Computer

Battle, Stafford. **The African-American Resource Guide to the Internet and Online Services,** New York: McGraw-Hill, 1996.

Index

ABOUT THE AUTHOR

Dr. Oneal Cleaven Sandidge is a licensed and ordained preacher who received ministerial direction under the direction of Rev. George Bolden, Jr. He was reared in Amherst County, Virginia. He is a member of the Timothy Baptist Church in Amherst County, Virginia where currently Rev. Horace Spears is the pastor. He has also been a member of the Salem Baptist Church, Atlanta, Georgia where Dr. Jasper Williams, Jr. is pastor.

Oneal holds the following degrees: Doctor of Ministry with specialization in Christian Education from Drew University, Madison, New Jersey; Master of Religion and American Education from Columbia University, New York, New York; Master of Arts in Christian Education from Howard University Divinity School, Washington, D.C. and a Bachelor of Arts in Elementary Education and Religion from a private college, Lynchburg College, Lynchburg, Virginia. He is a 1974 graduate of Amherst County High School in Amherst, Virginia. He has done further study at Virginia Union University, Richmond, Virginia and University of Virginia, Charlottesville, Virginia. In 1992, Oneal was selected and completed courses for the Merrill's Fellow at Harvard University, Cambridge, Massachusetts. In 1993, he was selected and completed graduate writing classes as Fellow for the Southside Virginia Writing Project, Virginia State University, Petersburg, Virginia.

Dr. Sandidge has taught middle school English and History, and all upper elementary subjects over a period of eight years. In addition, he has taught History of the Black Church at Piedmont Virginia Community College and Christian Education and other subjects at Virginia Seminary and College in Lynchburg, Virginia for a number of years. He is former Associate Professor of Christian Education at Beulah Heights Bible College in Atlanta, Georgia and served as Assistant Professor of Christian Education at Luther Rice Seminary in Atlanta, Georgia. He has lectured on various Christian education subjects at national and local levels, including Hampton Virginia Ministers' Conference for Christian Education, the United Methodist Church—national level, and the Dr. Donald Parson Ministries, prominent national lecturer in Chicago. He has written various articles including: **The Howard University Journal** "The Uniqueness of Black Preaching," and numerous articles in Christian Education journals and magazines such as **Church School Today.** He holds memberships in numerous clubs, including Kappa Delta Pi Honor Society, Columbia University. Oneal is author of Teacher Training in the African-American Church.

He has taught Curriculum Development in the National Baptist Convention, USA, Incorporated. He served as Minister of Education at the prominent Convent Avenue Baptist Church in New York City being responsible for seventy-five teachers, a superintendent, four department superintendents, eleven main ministries and about twenty-five sub ministries under the Board of Christian Education. He is married to Janice Cheryl Oliver. Children: Ieke Monique, and Jermaine Oneal Sandidge, and godson, Rev. Ronnie A. Clark.

For lectures/workshops in your city, contact:

AGENT FOR Dr. Oneal Sandidge
   4752 Elon Road
   Monroe, Virginia 24574